Reviews of Note
from colleagues and professionals

"A WONDROUS DIVERSITY OF VOICES EXPLORE THE ETHICS OF PSYCHOTHERAPY. Readers will find new research, original analyses, attention to crucial issues that have been historically neglected, and thoughtful challenges to widely held assumptions. . . . It's hard to imagine any newly practicing or well-seasoned clinician who would not benefit by engaging with the data, perspectives, experiences, and dilemmas that this book articulates with such force and clarity."
— Kenneth S. Pope, PhD, Diplomate in Clinical Psychology, Los Angeles, California

"A CHALLENGING CONTRIBUTION OFFERING SOME USEFUL FEMINIST PERSPECTIVES ON ETHICAL ISSUES. . . . This is the first publication of Dr. Mindy Benowitz's key, groundbreaking research on sexual contact between female clients and female therapists. . . . Dr. LaDue provides a unique contribution concerning Native American issues in therapy."
— Gary Richard Schoener, Licensed Psychologist and Executive Director, Walk-In Counseling Center, Minneapolis, Minnesota

"AN EXCELLENT SOURCE FOR THOSE INTERESTED IN MENTAL HEALTH ETHICS as well as for those committed to the teaching of such a crucial field. . . . Courageously reminds us that our honest approach of how much we still need to learn and research in the field of ethics will inspire us all to remain ethical no matter how difficult the professional circumstance might be."
— Silvia W. Olarte, MD, FAPA, Associate Clinical Professor of Psychiatry and Training Psycotherapist, New York Medical College

"Reflects a new level of maturity and sophistication in feminist therapy. It takes on the hard questions about power and responsibility of therapists, and deals with them forthrightly. IT OUGHT TO BECOME A PART OF EVERY PRACTICING THERAPIST'S WORKING LIBRARY."

— Judith Lewis Herman, MD, Department of Psychiatry, Harvard Medical School

Bringing Ethics Alive: Feminist Ethics in Psychotherapy Practice

Bringing Ethics Alive: Feminist Ethics in Psychotherapy Practice

Nanette K. Gartrell, MD
Editor

Bringing Ethics Alive: Feminist Ethics in Psychotherapy Practice, edited by Nanette K. Gartrell, was simultaneously issued by The Haworth Press, Inc., under the same title, as a special issue of the journal *Women & Therapy*, Volume 15, Number 1 1994, Nanette K. Gartrell, Editor.

Harrington Park Press
An Imprint of
The Haworth Press, Inc.
New York • London • Norwood (Australia)

1-56023-051-7

Published by

Harrington Park Press, 10 Alice Street, Binghamton, NY 13904-1580

Harrington Park Press is an imprint of The Haworth Press, Inc., 10 Alice Street, Binghamton, NY 13904-1580 USA.

Bringing Ethics Alive: Feminist Ethics in Psychotherapy Practice has also been published as
Women & Therapy, Volume 15, Number 1 1994.

The Haworth Press, Inc., 10 Alice Street, Binghamton, NY 13904-1580 USA

Library of Congress Cataloging-in-Publication Data

Bringing ethics alive : feminist ethics in psychotherapy practice / Nanette K. Gartrell, editor.
    p. cm.
    "Has also been published as Women & therapy, volume 1, number 1, 1994"–T.p. ver-
so.
    Includes bibliographical references.
    ISBN 1-56024-511-5 (alk. paper). – ISBN 1-56023-051-7 (alk. paper)
    1. Psychotherapy–Moral and ethical aspects. 2. Feminist ethics. 3. Feminist therapy–
Moral and ethical aspects. 4. Psychotherapy–Moral and ethical aspects–Study and
teaching. I. Gartrell, Nanette.
    [DNLM: 1. Psychotherapy. 2. Ethics, Professional. 3. Women. WM 420 B858 1994]
RC455.2.E8B75 1994
174' .2–dc20
DNLM/DLC
for Library of Congress
                                                                              93-44928
                                                                                   CIP

INDEXING & ABSTRACTING

Contributions to this publication are selectively indexed or abstracted in print, electronic, online, or CD-ROM version(s) of the reference tools and information services listed below. This list is current as of the copyright date of this publication. See the end of this section for additional notes.

- *Abstracts of Research in Pastoral Care & Counseling*, Loyola College, 7135 Minstrel Way, Suite 101, Columbia, MD 21045

- *Academic Index (on-line)*, Information Access Company, 362 Lakeside Drive, Foster City, CA 94404

- *Alternative Press Index*, Alternative Press Center, Inc., P.O. Box 33109, Baltimore, MD 21218

- *Bulletin Signaletique*, INIST/CNRS-Service Gestion des Documents Primaires, 2, allee du Parc de Brabois, F-54514 Vandoeuvre-les-Nancy, Cedex, France

- *Digest of Neurology and Psychiatry*, The Institute of Living, 400 Washington Street, Hartford, CT 06106

- *Expanded Academic Index,* Information Access Company, 362 Lakeside Drive, Forest City, CA 94404

- *Family Violence & Sexual Assault Bulletin*, Family Violence & Sexual Assault Institute, 1310 Clinic Drive, Tyler, TX 75701

- *Feminist Periodicals: A Current Listing of Contents*, Women's Studies Librarian-at-Large, 728 State Street, 430 Memorial Library, Madison, WI 53706

- *Higher Education Abstracts*, Claremont Graduate School, 740 North College Avenue, Claremont, CA 91711

(continued)

- *Index to Periodical Articles Related to Law*, University of Texas, 727 East 26th Street, Austin, TX 78705

- *Inventory of Marriage and Family Literature (online and hard copy)*, National Council on Family Relations, 3989 Central Avenue NE, Suite 550, Minneapolis, MN 55421

- *Mental Health Abstracts (online through DIALOG)*, IFI/Plenum Data Company, 3202 Kirkwood Highway, Wilmington, DE 19808

- *Periodical Abstracts, Research I* (general & basic reference indexing & abstracting data-base from University Microfilms International (UMI), 300 North Zeeb Road, P.O. Box 1346, Ann Arbor, MI 48106-1346), UMI Data Courier, P.O. Box 32770, Louisville, KY 40232-2770

- *Periodical Abstracts, Research II* (broad coverage indexing & abstracting data-base from University Microfilms International (UMI) 300 North Zeeb Road, P.O. Box 1346, Ann Arbor, MI 48106-1346), UMI Data Courier, P.O. Box 32770, Louisville, KY 40232-2770

- *Psychological Abstracts (PsycINFO)*, American Psychological Association, P.O. Box 91600, Washington, DC 20090-1600

- *Sage Family Studies Abstracts*, Sage Publications, Inc., 2455 Teller Road, Newbury Park, CA 91320

- *Social Work Research & Abstracts*, National Association of Social Workers, 750 First Street NW, 8th Floor, Washington, DC 20002

- *Studies on Women Abstracts*, Carfax Publishing Company, P.O. Box 25, Abingdon, Oxfordshire OX14 3UE, United Kingdom

- *Women Studies Abstracts*, Rush Publishing Company, P.O. Box 1, Rush, NY 14543

- *Women's Studies Index (indexed comprehensively)*, G.K. Hall & Co., 866 Third Avenue, New York, NY 10022

SPECIAL BIBLIOGRAPHIC NOTES

related to special journal issues (separates)
and indexing/abstracting

- [ ] indexing/abstracting services in this list will also cover material in the "separate" that is co-published simultaneously with Haworth's special thematic journal issue or DocuSerial. Indexing/abstracting usually covers material at the article/chapter level.

- [ ] monographic co-editions are intended for either non-subscribers or libraries which intend to purchase a second copy for their circulating collections.

- [ ] monographic co-editions are reported to all jobbers/wholesalers/approval plans. The source journal is listed as the "series" to assist the prevention of duplicate purchasing in the same manner utilized for books-in-series.

- [ ] to facilitate user/access services all indexing/abstracting services are encouraged to utilize the co-indexing entry note indicated at the bottom of the first page of each article/chapter/contribution.

- [ ] this is intended to assist a library user of any reference tool (whether print, electronic, online, or CD-ROM) to locate the monographic version if the library has purchased this version but not a subscription to the source journal.

- [ ] individual articles/chapters in any Haworth publication are also available through the Haworth Document Delivery Services (HDDS).

CONTENTS

ABOUT THE EDITOR

Nanette K. Gartrell, MD, is Associate Clinical Professor of Psychiatry at the University of California Medical School at San Francisco, where she teaches Ethics and Feminist Theory. Dr. Gartrell has been investigating and documenting sexual abuse by health professionals since 1982. Her other research interests include psychotherapy with lesbians, and lesbian parenting, and she is co-principal investigator of a longitudinal study of lesbians having children by alternative insemination. A reviewer for several professional journals, she is on the editorial board of *Women & Therapy.*

Preface

I first became interested in ethics when I was Chair of the American Psychiatric Association's Committee on Women in 1982. In that role, I took responsibility for advocating women's mental health issues within organized psychiatry. Shortly after assuming that position, I began to hear about sexual abuse of (primarily female) patients by (primarily male) psychiatrists. I realized that we would be unlikely to obtain funding for educational programs on psychiatric sexual abuse without documenting its prevalence. Therefore, I and colleagues Judith L. Herman and Silvia Olarte developed a questionnaire to survey the Association's membership. Our questionnaire was never approved for distribution. It created considerable anxiety with the Association, because many thought that documenting the prevalence of psychiatric sexual abuse would give the profession a bad reputation. We argued that abusive psychiatrists were more likely to damage the credibility of the profession, and that internal house cleaning might enhance psychiatry's public image.

Since the APA would not sponsor our study, we decided to conduct the survey independently, along with two Harvard statistician colleagues. Judith, Silvia and I published a series of papers on psychiatric sexual abuse (Gartrell, Herman, Olarte, Feinstein, & Localio, 1986; 1987; Gartrell, Herman, Olarte, Localio, & Feldstein, 1988; Gartrell, Olarte, & Herman, 1986; Herman, Gartrell, Olarte, Feldstein, & Localio, 1987). I and an interdisciplinary team of University of California at San Francisco colleagues recently documented the prevalence of sexual

Nanette K. Gartrell would like to thank Dorothy Allison for her editorial assistance in the preparation of this special issue.

[Haworth co-indexing entry note]: "Preface." Gartrell, Nanette K. Co-published simultaneously in *Women & Therapy* (The Haworth Press, Inc.) Vol. 15, No. 1, 1994, pp. *xi-xiii*; and: *Bringing Ethics Alive: Feminist Ethics in Psychotherapy Practice* (ed: Nanette K. Gartrell) The Haworth Press, Inc., 1994, pp. *xi-xiii*. Multiple copies of this article/chapter may be purchased from The Haworth Document Delivery Center [1-800-3-HAWORTH; 9:00 a.m. - 5:00 p.m. (EST)].

abuse by internists, obstetrician-gynecologists, surgeons and family practitioners.

Although my focus in medical and mental health ethics has been primarily limited to sexual exploitation, I was very pleased to have been asked to put together a special volume on Feminist Ethics. Editing this special edition seemed a perfect opportunity for me to broaden my interests to include other ethical concerns. Multicultural representation in authorship was my first priority, because any discussion of feminist ethics must incorporate diverse experiences due to race, ethnicity, class, and sexual orientation. I was fortunate that almost all of the women I invited to contribute articles had the time and interest to do so.

The articles in this volume are presented in two sections: Ethics in Theory, and Ethics in Practice. In the first section, Vasquez and Eldridge address the ethical responsibility for training programs to incorporate racism, sexism, heterosexism into their curricula. Beverly Greene reviews the principles which should be included in courses on ethics for psychotherapists in training.

Laura Brown develops a conceptual model for defining boundary violations in therapy.

In the Ethics in Practice section, Barbara Sanderson and I discuss sexual abuse of clients by women therapists. Mindy Benowitz follows with a summary of her doctoral dissertation comparing the experiences of women who were sexually abused by female therapists with women abused by male therapists. Pauline DeLozier gives a professional/personal account of sexual misconduct by a mental health professional. Hannah Lerman discusses her work on the ethics code of the Feminist Therapy Institute, and the difficulties she has observed in translating the code into practice. Robin LaDue brings this section to a close with an article on nonNative professionals' inappropriate use of Native spiritual practices or activities.

Many of the authors indicated to me that they were writing about issues which affected them profoundly and personally. I hope that the readers of this special volume will be as moved to consider the relevance of these topics to their own experiences as when I first read them.

Nanette K. Gartrell

REFERENCES

Gartrell, N., Herman, J., Olarte, S., Feldstein, M., & Localio, R. (1986) Psychiatrist-patient sexual contact: Results of a national survey, I: Prevalence. *American Journal of Psychiatry* 143(9) 1126-1131.

Gartrell, N., Herman, J., Olarte, S., Feldstein, M., Localio, R. (1987) Reporting Practices of psychiatrists who knew of sexual misconduct by colleagues. *American Journal Orthopsychiat.* 57(2) 287-295.

Gartrell, N., Herman, J., Olarte, S., Localio, R. & Feldstein, M. (1988) Psychiatric residents' sexual contact with educators and patients: Results of a national survey. *American Journal of Psychiatry* 145(6) 690-694.

Gartrell, N., Olarte, S., & Herman, J. (1986) Institutional resistance to self-study: A case report. In: A Burgess (Ed.) *Sexual exploitation of clients by health professionals*. Philadelphia: Praeger. 120-128.

Herman, J., Gartrell, N., Olarte, S., Feldstein, M., & Localio, R. (1987) Psychiatrist-patient sexual contact: Results of a national survey, II: Psychiatrists' attitudes. *American Journal of Psychiatry* 144(2) 164-169.

Bringing Ethics Alive:
Training Practitioners About Gender,
Ethnicity, and Sexual Orientation Issues

Melba J. T. Vasquez
Natalie S. Eldridge

Society is undergoing dramatic demographic shifts which will have substantial implications for the discipline of psychology and

Melba J. T. Vasquez, PhD, is a licensed psychologist employed in independent practice in Austin, TX. Dr. Vasquez has served on the American Psychological Association's Ethics Committee, its Board for the Advancement of Psychology in the Public Interest, and is currently a member of the Examination Committee of the Association of State and Provincial Psychology Boards.

Natalie S. Eldridge, PhD, is a licensed psychologist and Clinical Supervisor with the Boston University Counseling Center, and is Assistant Adjunct Clinical Professor in the Department of Developmental Studies and Counseling Psychology at Boston University. She is a feminist therapist with an independent practice in Boston, and serves as a member of the Lesbian Theory Group at the Stone Center, Wellesley College.

Correspondence may be addressed to Dr. Vasquez at 2901 Bee Cave Road, Box N, Austin, TX 78746.

[Haworth co-indexing entry note]: "Bringing Ethics Alive: Training Practitioners About Gender, Ethnicity, and Sexual Orientation Issues." Vasquez, Melba J.T., and Natalie S. Eldridge. Co-published simultaneously in *Women & Therapy* (The Haworth Press, Inc.) Vol. 15, No. 1, 1994, pp. 1-16; and *Bringing Ethics Alive: Feminist Ethics in Psychotherapy Practice* (ed: Nanette K. Gartrell) The Haworth Press, Inc., 1994, pp. 1-16. Multiple copies of this article/chapter may be purchased from The Haworth Document Delivery Center [1-800-3-HAWORTH; 9:00 a.m. - 5:00 p.m. (EST)].

1

the practice of mental health services. By the year 2000, one-third of the United States population will consist of ethnic minority populations. The number of women entering the workforce continues to increase. In 1970, 39% of the workforce were women. Today, women make up over 50% of the workforce. Currently, approximately 75% of the new workforce entries are women and ethnic minorities. The U.S. Labor Department predicts that the white male share of the labor force will drop to 39.4% by the year 2000 (U.S. Department of Labor, 1987). Although sexual orientation remains a controversial or silenced topic, a gay and lesbian presence is becoming increasingly visible in some domains, raising questions concerning employment benefit practices, recognition of domestic partnerships, and a widening definition of family and parenting. What are the mental health implications of such demographic changes? How will the practice, science and teaching of psychology and related fields be affected?

Psychology and related mental health professions are undergoing similar demographic shifts, reflecting the changes in society. In 1984, women outnumbered male graduates in psychology for the first time, becoming 50.1% of Ph.D. candidates. In 1990, 58% of Ph.D. graduates were women ("Task force examines," 1992). However, men continue to comprise the majority (60%) of the profession, and women comprise only 19% of tenured faculty ("Will feminization spell decline," 1992). The "feminization" of psychology is paralleled in other health and mental health professions. Most nurses and social workers are women, and the proportion of women among psychiatrists and other physicians is increasing rapidly.

Although ethnic minorities currently comprise one-fourth of the U.S. population, and while 20% of undergraduate psychology majors are ethnic minorities, only 11% go to graduate school for psychology and 9% graduate. The end result is that only 5% of all psychologists are ethnic minorities. Ethnic minorities make up only 5.3% of psychology faculty ("Adapt to diversity," 1992). This means that the ethnic minority presence in the profession is grossly underrepresented.

Representation of gays, lesbians and bisexuals in psychology and related fields is difficult to gauge. An increase in the number of mental health professionals who identify themselves as gay or lesbian has led to active new caucuses or divisions within professional organizations to attend to the needs of both the gay and lesbian professional, and the gay and lesbian populations each profession serves. These advocacy and support networks within professional organizations have encouraged professionals of all sexual orientations to be more gay affirmative in their understanding of lesbian and gay identity development, lifestyles, and therapeutic needs. Thus the concerns of gays and lesbians have a small, but increasingly significant, role in the mental health professions.

Demographic changes, both in society and those paralleled in the professions of mental health, have major implications for the kind of training and teaching needed in psychology, and in the training of therapeutic and other mental health services in particular. Are the mental health professions providing appropriate training to meet the needs of women, ethnic minorities, lesbian and gay men, and other diverse groups?

History of Psychology. According to Albee (1988), a former President of the American Psychological Association, psychology does not have an admirable record in educating students about the importance of social environmental factors in behavior. In fact, psychology often reflected blatant racism, sexism and heterosexism. G. Stanley Hall, for example, thought women were unsuitable for graduate and professional education because of intellectual deficiencies (although he sponsored several successful women graduate students). Albee also points out how several APA presidents believed that various non-White groups had inferior intelligence. Guthrie (1976) likewise documents the painful history of how social scientists, and psychologists in particular, conducted research based on racist premises. African American and Mexican American children were frequently tested with IQ and other tests constructed in a manner to ignore culture. Attempts were made to classify individuals to such categories as lip size, degree of hair waviness, head size, and to assume that bilingualism resulted in mental confusion. It took pioneers like George I. Sanchez (Guthrie, 1976) and "radical" anthropologists such as Franz Boas, Ruth Benedict, and Margaret Mead to challenge these belief systems (Albee, 1988). It took Evelyn Hooker's (1957) groundbreaking research to provide clear, dra-

matic empirical evidence that homosexuality per se is not patholog-
ical (Bayer and Hooker, 1968). These findings led to the revision of
the pathology model of homosexuality in the 1973 Diagnostic and
Statistical Manual of Mental Disorders (Second Edition).

In a recent survey, Tabachnick, Keith-Spiegel and Pope (1991)
found that few psychologists report ever teaching that certain races
are intellectually inferior (2%) or that homosexuality per se is path-
ological (5%). Yet, the exclusion of the emerging scholarship on
women, ethnic minorities, lesbian and gay populations and other
groups from the curriculum can have implications just as profound.
The general field of human psychological growth and development
has been taught from theories and research based largely on the
experiences of white, heterosexual men (Gilligan, 1982).

The end result of either the exclusion of information on diverse
populations or the promotion of erroneous, biased information in
the academic curriculum is that students do not learn about the
experiences of the majority of the utilizers of mental health services
(women, ethnic minorities, lesbians, and gay men). There exists a
growing body of psychological research focusing on various populations. Yet, the teaching of psychology has not kept up with the
new scholarship on women, ethnic minorities, and other diverse
groups.

Responsibilities of Academics. Many argue that attention to sociocultural issues such as gender, ethnicity, and sexual orientation, is
"fringe" and that such "special interest" issues should not be part
of the academic curriculum. Faculty members argue that inclusion
of such issues promotes "politically correct" positions of some
groups in psychology, and compromises academic freedom. We
would propose that inclusion of information about gender, ethnicity
and sexual orientation, with basis in psychological knowledge,
theory, and research is not only legitimate, important, and central to
human behavior, but is an ethical responsibility. In fact, the Ethical
Principles of Psychologists and Code of Conduct (American Psychological Association, 1992) includes a principle which underscores the responsibility to provide students with the most current
and accurate information possible. Principle 6.03a, "Accuracy and
Objectivity in Teaching," promotes that notion. It reads, "When
engaged in teaching or training, psychologists present psychologi-

cal information accurately and with a reasonable degree of objectivity" (Principle 6.03a, American Psychological Association, 1992, p. 1607).

Many faculty members, researchers, and clinicians are not sufficiently informed about gender, cultural and societal influences on particular groups. That lack of knowledge can lead to the promotion of faulty information, and to the development of faulty studies. For instance, too many researchers don't describe their subjects' racial or socioeconomic background in the studies. They often overlook the very powerful influence of the environment on research participants. Consequently, inappropriate generalizations are made about groups, and/or faulty assumptions are made. If professors then present these studies to students without appropriate cautions about the limitations or biases they hold, then students receive a biased foundation and faculty have failed to reach the ethical standard. In addition, students in applied programs (counseling, clinical and school psychology, social work, psychiatry) who have not been appropriately exposed to the sociocultural issues of gender, ethnicity and sexual orientation may commit critical therapeutic errors.

In teaching and promoting therapeutic interventions, for instance, it is important to note that the behaviors most beneficial to women's health and mental health are not always the same as those that benefit men. Andrea Solarz, of the Federation of Behavioral, Psychological and Cognitive Sciences, is cited in an article on gaps in research on women as providing two reasons which account for the differences. One is that the organic and chemical systems with which behavior interacts are different for women and men. Second, the system of social pressures and rewards is not the same for women as for men ("Hearing pinpoints gaps," 1991). While the amount of overlap between the sexes is far greater than the differences between them, graduate study must include accurate information about critical differences, and how these differences affect social and therapeutic needs.

In counseling and therapy courses, instructors teach how interventions must be applied according to the needs of individuals. Knowledge of the client's sociocultural experience is critical to applying the appropriate intervention. For example, for those who teach behavioral courses relevant to work with addictive behaviors, it is important to know that many people abuse substances to repress traumatic childhood experiences, including sexual and physical abuse and incest, and that up to 75% of chemically dependent women have reported incidence of sexual abuse, according to one study ("Hearing pinpoints gaps," 1991). Models of intervention with addictive behaviors should thus be planned in order to address those traumatic experiences. If these experiences are not addressed, women especially will be underserved.

Incorporation of information on gender, cultural, and sexual orientation in teaching and training is not only an issue of competence and ethical responsibility. Programs which incorporate a broader diversity in their curriculum, and in all aspects of their research, training, and practice have been described as having more vitality, relevance, and quality. James Jones, who has been Director of the American Psychological Association's Minority Fellowship Program for fifteen years, has had the opportunity to work with research and applied programs whose students receive fellowships. He describes how ". . . the beneficiaries of focused attention on critical empirical issues of race, or development of practice skills with clients who are culturally or linguistically different are not just those ethnic or racial students whose presence instigates reformulation, but white students and faculty as well who begin to learn the ways and extent to which psychological knowledge and practice have bearing (across all) human behavior" ("We should affirm diversity," 1991).

A more inclusive psychology will indeed have a number of important beneficial effects on students and faculty. Bronstein and Quina (1988) describe how important it is for more students to be aware of the extent to which traditional psychological theory has been developed by and about White heterosexual majority-culture men, taking little account of women and minorities or regarding them as "deviant or deficient." Herek, Kimmel, Amaro, and Melton (1991) point out that most scientific research in the social and behavioral sciences has ignored sexual orientation and behavior or uncritically adopted societal prejudices against gay and bisexual populations. Practitioners have also been found to frequently provide biased, inadequate, or inappropriate care to lesbians and gay men (Garnets, Hancock, Cochran, Goodchilds, & Peplau, 1991). It is important for students to realize that scientific study and the interpretations of findings is almost never "objective" and is influenced by personal or political ideology. Our assumptions and our theories shape the questions we ask and thus the answers we get. A standard curriculum for those trained to deliver mental health services should promote cultural, social and gender awareness. Women, lesbians, ethnic minorities, and other diverse groups together make up the majority of all clients. Faculty bear an ethical responsibility to promote accurate knowledge about these groups. A more inclusive psychology can only have a positive effect on students, on the discipline, and on the practice of psychology and mental health.

Perspectives and Resources on the Implementation of Change. Incorporation of sociocultural issues in the study of human behavior is best implemented at both the graduate and the undergraduate levels. One of the key dilemmas in implementing curriculum change by incorporating sociocultural issues such as gender, ethnicity, and sexual orientation, is whether to integrate such information into the standard curriculum courses, or whether to develop separate courses to focus on particular populations. Advantages and disadvantages exist with both approaches, but the general consensus is that both approaches may be legitimate, and even appropriate.

An integrated curricula is best implemented when instructors have the willingness and ability to address diversity in a knowledgeable manner. Certainly, at the graduate level, courses on models of therapeutic intervention would include feminist, multicultural and gay affirmative theory and therapy. Brown and Root (1990) provide a collective group of diverse topics on feminist and multicultural therapy issues at a high level of theoretical conceptualization. Comas-Diaz and Greene (in press) have edited a book on psychotherapy with women of color, which provides a rich array of indepth understanding of various ethnic groups. Pedersen, Draguns, Lonner and Trimble (1989) have also edited a resource on multicultural counseling.

Courses which focus on human development should incorporate the two major forces on the new scholarship of women. Jordan, Kaplan, Miller, Stiver and Surrey (1991) have promoted a new scholarship on women's development, which focuses on the "self-in-relation" model. This model promotes a description of women's development as reflecting the capacity and need to maintain connection with others. The published work describing this model reflects earlier writings which do not adequately address the diversity of women's experiences along ethnic and sexual orientation dimensions. In a special lecture sponsored by the American Psychological Association in collaboration with the Smithsonian, Laura Brown ("Lectures at Smithsonian," 1992) described a second approach to understanding women's development, which she calls feminist social constructionism. She described how the proponents of this model challenge the model proposed by Jordan et al. (1991), and ask whether there is such a thing as women's unique developmental path. They look at the various ways in which women may develop, and especially focus on environmental influences. Both models and approaches to studying the development of women form the new scholarship of the psychology of women. Lott (1987) also provides a rich resource about the experiences through which gender is learned and maintained by contemporary girls and women in society. This resource can be easily adapted for both graduate and undergraduate level. We would posit that, regardless of the model or approach to human development, the educator must be sure that issues of diversity along gender, ethnic and sexual orientation dimensions are discussed.

Faculty have the responsibility to understand and convey the psychological impact of the various and complex experiences of women, ethnic minorities and lesbian and gay individuals in society. An assessment instructor, for example, might demonstrate how phenomena associated with gender and culture can influence the assessment process in various ways. In addressing the "gender gap" (the controversial differential between male and female scores) on cognitive ability tests, an instructor should be able to provide the complex analysis as to whether and to what extent the differences are due to test construction and administration, or whether the differences are due to socialization processes which discourage girls from "academic risk taking," necessary for the development of problem-solving skills ("Gender gap," 1991). While some believe that tests construction and administration are not a problem, others point to studies that demonstrate that both boys and girls, and especially girls, perform much better when achievement tests are administered by examiners who are of the same gender as the test taker (Pedersen, Shinedling & Johnson, as cited in Pope & Vasquez, 1991). A competent assessment instructor would be able to provide information for discussion of these complex issues.

The inclusion of principles developed for the delivery of services for diverse populations in ethics courses is also an important responsibility. For example, the "Principles concerning the counseling and therapy of women" (American Psychological Association, 1978) and the "Guidelines for providers of psychological services to ethnic, linguistic, and culturally diverse populations" (American Psychological Association, 1993) are valuable and instructive guidelines. Garnets et al. (1991) report results of a survey of psychologists which clearly demonstrate a wide variation in their adherence to a standard of unbiased practice with gay men and lesbians, and lays the groundwork for models of education and training in this area. Specific guidelines for ethical practice with these populations have not yet been developed.

Separate courses about a particular population allow for fuller and more in-depth exploration of knowledge. The risks may involve: isolation of knowledge; isolation of the instructors (frequently women or ethnic minorities); majority group instructors may assume the specialized course covers all issues, and thus not include such material in their courses. Additionally, taking such courses can overload an already loaded curriculum for students. However, students often enjoy and find these courses to be highly meaningful for scholarly importance as well as for personal impact (Bronstein & Quina, 1988).

Whether teaching in integrated courses or separate ones, potential errors are committed when statistical group differences are treated as categorical, or when groups are placed in opposition (for example, heterosexual vs. homosexual) for purposes of comparison (Bronstein & Quina, 1988). Bronstein and Quina (1988), in their edited book which serves as a resource for teaching about diversity, attempts to ". . . recast the perspective away from group differences and insidious comparisons, toward themes and variations among and within races, genders, cultures, sexual orientations, and life circumstances such as disability or poverty" (p. 8). They recommend that students be reminded that differences among individuals within any group (gender, ethnicity, etc.) are always greater than differences between groups. A suggested approach is to focus on individual lives and experiences through interviews, autobiographies or novels as illustrations of the impact of race, gender, and sexual orientation, rather than as representative of all members of that group. Many valuable suggestions for approaching the teaching of both integrated and separate courses are offered in the Bronstein and Quina (1988) resource published by the American Psychological Association.

In addition, there are several journals (such as *Psychology of Women Quarterly, Sex Roles, Hispanic Journal of Behavioral Science, Journal of Black Psychology, Journal of Homosexuality*), a range of textbooks, teaching resources such as videotapes, films and course syllabi devoted to the psychology of women, ethnic minorities, and lesbian and gay men. The knowledge and scholarship are available, and the body of work will likely continue to grow. The yearly conventions of mental health organizations (American Psychological Association, American Psychiatric Association, National Association of Social Workers) are one place where convention workshops, symposia, and videos are presented which focus on the growing body of psychological research focusing on various populations. Women's Studies, Black Studies, and Chicano Studies associations also meet yearly to exchange scholarly research, theory and knowledge.

Teaching Styles and Attitudes. In addition to the ethical responsibility to provide accurate and complete knowledge, faculty have a responsibility to know how students learn. As more women enter the mental health fields, and as ethnic minorities increase numbers, it is important for faculty to understand that women and ethnic minorities may learn differently than white males. Harris (1988) describes a "reclaiming of a tradition of scholarship which goes back to Plato and Pestalozzi, to Mary Wollstonecraft and Catherine Beecher, a tradition of examining the relation between women and education" (p. 6-7). Harris describes how many, including Jean Baker Miller, Carol Gilligan and Nancy Chodorow are examining ways in which women are educated. In particular, Harris (1988) proposes a continuing focus on the processes and procedures through which women students might be taken more seriously in the administration, supervision, context, and sociology of education, and in the creation of new language, remedial and compensatory programs.

The problem can be partly described in the context of gender equity issues, beginning at young ages. The report of a recent survey by the American Association of University Women confirmed the need for education reform which incorporates gender equity, beginning in elementary school. The report ("Self-esteem gender gap," 1991) described how girls experience a significantly larger drop in self-esteem during adolescence than boys. At ages 8 and 9, 60% of girls were confident and assertive and felt positive about themselves, compared to 67% of boys. But over the next eight years, girls' self-esteem fell 31 points–only 29% of high school girls felt positive about themselves. During the same period, boys' self-worth dropped 21 points–leaving 46% of high school boys with high self-esteem. The gender gap of 17 points is of concern because it lowers girls' confidence in their abilities and limits their career aspirations. Interestingly, many more black girls retained their self-esteem in high school than either white or Hispanic girls, which the researchers attributed to family and community reinforcement. But black adolescent girls exhibited significant drops in positive feelings about their teachers and school work as they got older. Some hypothesize that while family support appears to bolster black girls' self-esteem, and to reject the negative things that are said about them in society, academic self-esteem declines. Hispanic girls were much less confident and positive about themselves than black girls, and between elementary school and high school their confidence and self-esteem plummeted farther than either black or white girls. These findings confirm those of Gilligan, Brown and Rogers of the Harvard Project on the Psychology of Women and the Development of Girls ("Self-esteem gender gap," 1991). Gilligan's findings describe how girls found that they face a conflict between staying in touch with their own beliefs and feelings–for example, with their view of their own capabilities–and adjusting to the reality of how other people view them. In an invited address on diversity, Jacquelynne Eccles ("Parents' attitude key," 1991) describes how parents' attitudes and expectations and classroom environments can help or hinder girls' self-confidence in math and science. In both contexts, high-performing boys get the most academic attention, and the typically well-behaved high-performing girls get very little attention.

Many have described how the culture in the educational system is symbolic of the highly individualistic and competitive values in society. A gender analysis forces us to be aware that we are living in a culture that has been constructed from the point of view of male life-experience. The "social construction of reality," in which men have been the chief actors, may not promote the best learning environment for women or for ethnic minorities.

For example, Elbow (1973) describes how women are often less validated in classroom settings because they are not taught to be good at the "doubting game." Doubters question everything; they are argumentative, competitive, and always looking for the flaw, fallacy, or inconsistency in what someone is saying. In contrast, believers believe all assertions, listen carefully and try to understand the point of view being expressed. Believers are flexible, supporting, cooperative and actively exploring the ideas of another. Yet, those who play the "doubting" game are often more validated because the doubting game is the game in power in most classrooms. In the educational model of power over others, an argumentative, competitive and critical climate often leads to a "chilly" climate for many women and ethnic minorities in the classroom, who are more likely to take the roles of "believers" than "doubters" (Belenky, Clinchy, Goldberger, & Tarule, 1986).

Another vehicle for learning is the use of role models or mentors. The very existence of and opportunity to experience a variety of successful exemplars of one's chosen field, while in the approach or training phases of a career, can have a transformative effect on the student/trainee. We have already discussed the disproportionate presence of women and ethnic minorities in the field of psychology. What about role models for lesbian, gay and bisexual students who need to see themselves reflected in their professional models and teachers?

Lesbian, gay and bisexual teachers are as invisible as the greater gay and lesbian populations. They often lead secretive lives in their schools or professions because they believe that identifying themselves to students, colleagues, or parents of students would result in the loss of job or loss of credibility within their professions. These fears are real, as employment rights are not protected on the basis of sexual orientation except in a handful of states or cities (Griffin, 1992). Even in a university setting, the pressure to remain closeted is great. The vulnerability and competitive nature of the tenure process, and the unfortunate tendency of professionals in the mental health fields to pathologize differences, can lead to a very unsupportive environment for coming out. Even those who are self-identified to their colleagues must face the inequity of treatment by the university, where they are prohibited from extending health, educational, or other benefits to their partners or non-biological children they are raising, as same-sex families are not afforded legal recognition. This leads to a reinforcement of the stigma of difference on a daily basis.

Sekaran and Kassner (1992) describe how educating a diverse population calls for complex, multidimensional perspectives and new models of training in higher education. They identify problems which impede progress for women and minorities (as faculty and as students) which stem from the university structure (tokenism, the old male tenure model, inflexibility of the system, exclusion from networks), from the university processes (teaching and service loads, salary inequity, degrading positions headed by minority women, allocation of resources predominantly to male faculty), and from group structures and process (attitudes and behaviors). The authors provide suggestions for improvement (recruiting, changing the reward system, creating the organizational culture, deploying a special recruiter, allocating a central reserve, ensuring equity, reexamining tenure time frames, and creating an office for Women's Professional Advancement). Leong, Snodgrass and Gardner III (1992) propose suggestions for creating a "gender-positive environment" in higher education. They describe such an environment as one in which the dominant value set "luxuriates" in diversity and novelty. In this environment, all individuals are able to grow and be rewarded for their contributions.

The classroom climate, whether at the elementary level, or in higher education, is currently viewed as "chilly," and even detrimental to gays, women and ethnic minorities. No one solution is promoted here. Educational reform is an extensive and complex process. However, teachers, instructors and faculty can be sensitive to the realities that women and ethnic minorities may have a tendency to learn more effectively in an environment which validates learning through cooperation, support, and helping others rather than attacking, arguing, and competing.

Those who teach and train must also be aware that we all have a tendency to devalue women's work, behavior, and accomplishments. Women's success is often attributed to luck, lack of difficulty, or romantic or sexual influences over others, rather than to women's competencies (Leong, Snodgrass, & Gardner III, 1992).

CONCLUSIONS

No longer can academics view the study of women, ethnic minority, and gay and lesbian development, as "fringe," as low order of scholarly endeavor, or as "politicization" of the university. Incorporating the content of diverse groups in psychology, and other social science and mental health related courses is an ethical responsibility, especially as the research continues to evolve. The impact of a more inclusive psychology on students and on the discipline and practice of psychology and mental health can be powerful and positive. Examination of teaching methods, styles, and attitudes is a challenge which faculty cannot afford to ignore. A decided shift in the demographic composition of American society is underway. It is a basic tenet of open systems theory that a change in any part of the system will affect other parts of the system. The rate of change is such that increased diversity is quickly effecting all major institutions, including higher education, psychology, and the mental health field. Our ethical responsibilities will hopefully guide us in making the adjustments necessary for change.

REFERENCES

Adapt to diversity or risk irrelevance, field warned. (1992, February). *APA Monitor, 23*, 44.

Albee, G.W. (1988). Foreword. In P.A. Bronstein & K. Quina (Eds.), *Teaching a psychology of people: Resources for gender and sociocultural awareness.* Washington, D.C.: American Psychological Association.

American Psychological Association. (1992). Ethical principles of psychologists and code of conduct. *American Psychologist. 47*, 1597-1611.

American Psychological Association. (1993b). *Guidelines for psychological services to ethnic, linguistic, and culturally diverse populations. American Psychologist, 48*. 45-48.

American Psychological Association. (1978). *Principles concerning the counseling and therapy of women.* Washington, D. C.: Author.

Bayer, R. (1981). *Homosexuality and American Psychiatry: The Politics of Diagnosis.* New York: Basic Books, pp. 49-52.

Belenky, M.G., Clinchy, B. M., Goldberger, N. R., & Tarule, J. M. (1986). *Women's ways of knowing: The development of self, voice and mind.* New York: Basic Books.

Bronstein, P. A. & Quina, K. (Eds.). (1988). Perspectives on gender balance and cultural diversity in the teaching of psychology. In Bronstein, P. A. & Quina, K. (Eds.) *Teaching a psychology of people: Resources for gender and sociocultural awareness.* Washington, D.C.: American Psychological Association, 3-11.

Bronstein, P. A. & Quina, K. (Eds.). (1988). *Teaching a psychology of people: Resources for gender and sociocultural awareness.* Washington, D.C.: American Psychological Association.

Brown, L. S. & Root, M. P. P. (Eds.) (1990). *Diversity and complexity in feminist therapy.* Binghamton, NY: The Haworth Press, Inc.

Comas-Diaz, L. & Greene, B. (in press) (Eds.). *Women of Color and Mental Health: The Integration of Race, Gender, and Culture into Treatment.* New York: Guilford Press.

Elbow, P. (1973). *Writing without teachers.* London: Oxford University Press.

Garnets, L., Hancock, K. A., Cochran, S. D., Goodchilds, J., & Peplau, L. A. (1991). Issues in psychotherapy with lesbians and gay men. *American Psychologist, 46*, 964-972.

Gender gap on tests examined at meeting. (1991, December). *APA Monitor, 22*, 16.

Gilligan, C. (1982). *In a different voice.* Cambridge, MA: Harvard University Press.

Griffin, P. (1992). Lesbian and gay educators: Opening the classroom closet. *Empathy, 3*, 25-28.

Guthrie, R.V. (1976). *Even the rat was white: A historical view of psychology.* New York: Harper & Row.

Harris, M. (1988). *Women and teaching: Themes for a spirituality of pedagogy.* New York: Paulist Press.

Hearing pinpoints gaps in research on women. (1991, June). *APA Monitor, 22*, 8.

Herek, G. M., Kimmel, D. C., Amaro, H., & Melton, G. B. (1991). Avoiding heterosexual bias in psychological research. *American Psychologist, 46*, 957-963.

Hooker, E. (1968). Homosexuality. In *The International Encyclopedia of the Social Sciences.* Macmillan Co., & The Free Press, pp. 222-233.

Jackson, J. H. (1992). Trials, tribulations and triumphs of minorities in psychology:

Reflections at Century's end. *Professional Psychology: Research and Practice, 23,* 80-86.

Jordan, J. V., Kaplan, A. G., Miller, J. B., Stiver, I. P., & Surrey, J. L. (1991). *Women's growth in connection: Writings from the Stone Center.* New York: Guilford Press.

Lectures at Smithsonian examine human life cycle. (1992, March). *APA Monitor, 23,* 4.

Leong, F. T. L., Snodgrass, C. R. & Gardner III, W. L. (1992). Management education: Creating a gender-positive environment. In U. Sekaran, & F. T. L. Leong (Eds.), *Womanpower: Managing in times of demographic turbulence.* Newbury Park, CA: Sage.

Lott, B. (1987). *Women's Lives: Themes and variations in gender learning.* Pacific Grove, CA: Brooks/Cole.

Miller, J.B. (1976). *Toward a new psychology of women.* Boston: Beacon Press.

Parents' attitude key to girls' achievement. (1991, October). *APA Monitor, 22,* 16.

Pedersen, D., Shinedling, M., & Johnson, D. (1975). Effects of sex of examiner and subject on children's quantitative test performance. In R. K. Unger and F. Denmark (Eds.), *Women: dependent or independent variable?* (pp. 410-472). New York: Psychological Dimensions.

Pedersen, P. Draguns, J., Lonner, W., & Trimble, J. (1989) (Eds.). *Counseling Across Cultures* (3rd ed.). Honolulu: University of Hawaii Press.

Pope, K. S., & Vasquez, M.J.T. (1991). Ethics in psychotherapy and counseling: A practical guide for psychologists. San Francisco: Jossey-Bass.

Sekaran, U., & Kassner, M. (1992). University systems for the 21st century: Proactive adaptation. In U. Sekaran & F. T. L. Leong (Eds.) *Womanpower: Managing in times of demographic turbulence* (pp. 163-191). Newbury Park: Sage.

Self-esteem gender gap widens in adolescence. (1991, April). *APA Monitor, 22,* 29.

Tabachnick, B. G., Keith-Spiegel, P., & Pope, K. (1991). Ethics of Teaching: Beliefs and behaviors of psychologists as educators. *American Psychologist, 46,* 506-515.

Task force examines issues raised by feminization of field. (1992, February). *APA Monitor, 23,* 47.

U.S. Department of Labor. (1987). Workforce 2000: Work and Workers for the 21st Century. (Hudson Institute Report). Washington, D.C.: Author.

We should affirm diversity to ease race bias, benefit society as a whole. (1991, February). *APA Monitor, 22,* 37.

Will feminization spell decline for field? (1991, October). *APA Monitor, 22,* 12.

Teaching Ethics in Psychotherapy

Beverly Greene

The practice of psychotherapy takes place under a highly speci-
fied set of conditions and circumstances which make it necessary to
develop guidelines to protect the client, third party interests and the
therapist. Despite the highly personal nature of the content of communications between the therapist and client, theirs is not a social
relationship. Nor does it fit strictly within the framework of routine
commercial or business relationships. There is usually an expectation on the part of the consumer, who is often most vulnerable in
this arrangement, that a therapist be professionally competent and
trustworthy (Keith-Spiegel & Koocher, 1985). While desired out-
comes in psychotherapy cannot be routinely guaranteed, it is presumed that the therapist, if she cannot be helpful, will certainly do
no harm. It therefore becomes necessary to maintain an explicit and
mutually agreed upon set of standards which clarify the responsibilities and rights of the client and the therapist in this arrangement, as
well as a formal and routine method for communicating those standards to persons who plan to engage in the practice of psychotherapy.
While there are subtle differences between the philosophies of
distinct mental health disciplines, most maintain formal standards

Beverly Greene, PhD, is Associate Clinical Professor of Psychology at St.
John's University, Jamaica, NY, where she teaches ethics and cultural diversity in
psychological services, and is Co-editor of *Women of color and mental health*.
She has a private psychotherapy practice in Brooklyn, NY.
Correspondence may be addressed to the author at the Dept. of Psychology, St.
John's University, Jamaica, NY 11439.

[Haworth co-indexing entry note]: "Teaching Ethics in Psychotherapy." Greene, Beverly. Co-published simultaneously in *Women & Therapy* (The Haworth Press, Inc.) Vol. 15, No. 1, 1994, pp. 17-27;
and *Bringing Ethics Alive: Feminist Ethics in Psychotherapy Practice* (ed: Nanette K. Gartrell) The
Haworth Press, Inc., 1994, pp. 17-27. Multiple copies of this article/chapter may be purchased from The
Haworth Document Delivery Center [1-800-3-HAWORTH; 9:00 a.m. - 5:00 p.m. (EST)].

of appropriate conduct which they require of their members. Mandatory courses in ethics and professional issues are the typical means by which this information is communicated to psychotherapists in training. A general framework for organizing such a course, including a review of major ethical principles deemed significant across mental health disciplines (AACD, 1988; AAMFT, 1991; AMHCA, 1987; APsyAnAssn, 1983; APA, 1989; APA, 1992; CPSBP, 1987; FTI, 1990; NASW, 1990), available resources which may be used to augment course lectures, and exercises which facilitate both the communication and understanding of this material will serve as the focus of this article.

ETHICAL PRINCIPLES

The major objective of ethics courses in psychotherapy is to familiarize therapists in training with the current standards of professional practice which serve to guide professional conduct in a variety of settings. To accomplish this, the major ethical principles or codes relevant to the conduct of psychotherapy in a specific discipline or across disciplines should be reviewed. Such a review should include an understanding of the conditions that give rise to ethical dilemmas for specific principles and the development of strategies for resolving those dilemmas which meet the highest current standards of professional conduct. Detailed and diverse examples of cases which exemplify ethical dilemmas may be found in Ethics Committee of APA (1988), Hall (1987), Keith-Spiegel and Koocher (1985), Lakin (1991) and Pope and Vetter (1991).

Ethical dilemmas run the gamut of diversity and complexity, hence few principles can be applied unilaterally as exact answers to problems. Rather, they may be considered guidelines or a framework to be used in making decisions with the overriding goal of doing that which best serves the client's interest.

ORGANIZING A BASIC CONTRACT FOR SERVICES

In keeping with the need to maintain the clarity and boundaries of the psychotherapy relationship, the course must allow for instruction on the importance of defining the parameters and structure of therapy and communicating them to the client in a manner that the client can understand. Some disciplines express a clear preference for a written contract or informed consent which explicitly states the goals of treatment, how they are to be accomplished, how progress toward those goals is to be evaluated, risks of treatment to the client and both the client and therapist's rights (Keith-Spiegel & Koocher, 1985; Pope & Vasquez, 1991). Whether written or verbal, most disciplines agree on the need for a formal discussion of the parameters of the agreement and its basic elements which should also include, but are not exclusive to, explanations of fee structure, how payment is to be made, policy regarding third party providers, appointment schedule, cancellation policy, availability during emergencies, disclosure of credentials, level of training and scope of expertise, and under what circumstances treatment would be terminated either at the client or therapist's initiation. It is presumed that an open discussion of these elements of treatment will facilitate the client's ability to make an informed decision about whether or not to proceed with treatment and/or with the specific practitioner. Bednar, Bednar, Lambert and Waite (1991), Vesper and Brock (1991) and Zuckerman and Guyett (1991) provide examples of contracts and informed consent agreements with contents which are consistent with the ethical requirements of most mental health disciplines.

PROFESSIONAL COMPETENCE

Consistent with the ethical mandate to provide services which are in the client's best interests, therapists in training must become familiar with the appropriate scope and limits of their professional expertise, of the requirement to practice within those limits and to accurately represent their training and credentials (Corey, Corey & Callanan, 1993; Howard, 1990; Keith-Spiegel & Koocher, 1985; Pope & Vasquez, 1991; Thompson, 1990; Vesper & Brock, 1991). Training in this area must include current requirements for professional licensing, certification and specialized credentials relevant to the practice of psychotherapy for specific disciplines in specific geographic locales. The practitioner's responsibilities in responding to the inquiries of professional boards and committees as well as the usefulness of these boards and professional associations as resources when the practitioner wishes to gain assistance in clarifying an ethical question should be explored as well.

Mental health disciplines previously referred to in this paper maintain that their members may not treat clients whose problems are outside the realm of the practitioner's training and/or experience (Corey, Corey & Callanan, 1993). Hence it is important to include instruction on the specialized role of other mental health, medical, and nonmedical specialties as well as their appropriate use in consultation or referral. It is particularly important for non-medical practitioners to understand the range of circumstances when referral for psychiatric, neurological or other medical consultation is appropriate to the client's care, as well as when it is considered a standard part of treatment. A brief review of physical conditions which may be expressed as symptoms of emotional distress and vice versa may be used to assist one's thinking when faced with the question of when it is important to make such referrals.

Special standards of competence may be required when working with members of distinct racial and cultural groups, lesbians and gay men, economically impoverished clients as well as high risk clients (Bednar et al., 1991). Ibrahim and Arredondo (1986) discuss proposed ethical standards for cross cultural counseling preparation. Cayleff (1986), Corey et al. (1993), and Hall (1987) review a range of ethical and cultural issues which may arise when counseling women, lesbians and gay men and members of distinct cultural groups, while Pedersen and Marsella (1982) examine current ethical guidelines to determine if they are sensitive to the special issues raised in cross cultural counseling and therapies. Keith-Spiegel and Koocher (1985) provide a range of case examples.

CONFIDENTIALITY

One of the foundations of the psychotherapeutic relationship is based on the assumption that verbal and written communications between the client and therapist are confidential and will not be divulged without the client's formal written consent. Instruction in this area must include the extent to which such communications are protected by law in the state of practice and the circumstances which ethically or legally compel the therapist to divulge the content of such communications (Conte, Plutchik, Picard & Toksoz, 1989; Corey et al., 1993; Keith-Spiegel & Koocher, 1985; Kentsmith, Salladay & Miya, 1986; Pope & Bajt, 1988; Pope & Vasquez, 1991). As clients may not undo what they have told a therapist after it is said, most of the aforementioned authors favor that therapists in training be encouraged to communicate the limits of confidentiality at the very outset of treatment and many suggest that this be done in writing. Zuckerman and Guyett (1991) offer a range of suggestions on how to do this clearly and effectively.

Instruction in this area should also include a review of requirements for the maintenance and disposal of written communications, notes or records. This discussion should include specific guidelines regarding what must be included in formal records and what should not be included, who owns the records, who has access and under what circumstances a practitioner may be required to surrender records to a third party with or without the client's consent. As the latter often occurs when records are subpoenaed, appropriate procedures for responding to court requests for records, testimony or other privileged material within the practitioner's locale should be reviewed (see Keith-Spiegel & Koocher, 1985 and Vesper & Brock, 1991).

Course content must address the professional responsibility to breach confidentiality when doing so is the only way to identify clients who are a danger to themselves or others and to warn potential victims of the danger such clients pose to them. This may be accomplished by review of case rulings which established legal precedents, the most prominent of which is the duty to warn (Tarasoff, 1976). Corey et al. (1993) and Keith-Spiegel and Koocher (1985) review these cases in detail and provide discussions of their clinical implications as well. In this author's experience, it is important to reinforce the distinction between the requirement to breach confidentiality to prevent harm as opposed to the therapist's motivation to see a client punished for past transgressions even though there is no clear danger to an identifiable person in the present.

Many states consider psychotherapists "mandated reporters" and compel them to report suspicions of child abuse, even if it violates the confidentiality of therapy. Some states impose criminal penalties on mandated reporters who fail to report their suspicions.

A review of these regulations should be included in course material if laws in the state require such action of therapists. Such a review should convey the circumstances under which reports are to be made and to whom.

CONFLICTS OF INTEREST

A conflict of interest in psychotherapy occurs when the therapist engages in some other significant relationship with the client, or has done so in the past, thus confusing the boundaries of their professional relationship. This may also lead to a misuse of the power inherent in the role of the therapist, addressing the therapist rather than the client's needs. Such conflicts may occur if the therapist engages in business and/or social and therapy relationships simultaneously creating dual or overlapping relationships. Conflicts of interest are not limited to personal relationships but may also occur when the therapist harbors attitudes, biases, or values which may be poorly understood and interfere with the therapist's ability to view the client with objectivity and respect. The therapist's clarification of their own values and limits is an important ingredient in limiting their negative effects.

Training of psychotherapists must include material which facilitates a heightened level of awareness of the power dynamics in the therapy relationship, specifically the power at one's disposal as a therapist in encounters with clients. The feminist therapy literature has most eloquently and thoroughly explored this area, particularly the potential for traditional therapies, if unmodified, to perpetuate the inequality in the relationship (Adleman & Barrett, 1990; Brown, 1990; Lerman & Rigby, 1990; Lerman & Porter, 1990). Inclusion of this material enriches the discussion of this complex issue.

Mental health ethics codes generally consider dual relationships in psychotherapy to be unethical with the assumption that they are ultimately destructive to clients (Keith-Spiegel & Koocher, 1985; Kentsmith et al., 1986; Kitchner, 1988; Lakin, 1991; Pope, 1991; Thompson, 1990; Vesper & Brock, 1991). While most therapists in training can understand why sexual/romantic relationships are harmful to clients and represent the most flagrant abuse of the therapist's power, they are often less certain about how bartering, business, teacher-therapist, social, and other apparently innocuous departures from the formality of the professional relationship may be just as harmful. It may be helpful to assist them in appreciating that the most egregious violations of boundaries do not generally begin that way. Their origins may be found in innocent exchanges of favors, gifts, and meetings outside of therapy which facilitate rather than mitigate against a further erosion of the boundaries in the relationship. This erosion of boundaries ultimately leads to changes in expectations and confusion within the therapy relationship. This does not mean that any violation of boundaries automatically results in the most extreme departure. Rather, the most extreme departures usually begin in behavior which may appear to be innocent. It is acknowledged that in some instances it may be impossible for the therapist and client to avoid some overlap in their lives. What must be communicated however is that the therapist should not seek or create situations which increase the probability of such overlap; rather she is expected to behave in ways which minimize it (Gartrell, 1992; Keith-Spiegel & Koocher, 1985; Pope & Vasquez, 1991).

A range of resources on therapist's sexual involvement with clients and their harmful effects includes Bouhoutsos (1985), Brown (1988), Pope and Vetter (1991), Sonne (1985) and Keith-Spiegel and Koocher (1985). Brown (1990), Shopland and VandeCreek (1991) and Vasquez (1991) review the harmful effects of sexual relationships with former clients and the rationales for considering such activity unethical. Despite ethical prohibitions, sexual relationships between client and therapist persist. Borys and Pope (1989), Gartrell (1986), Herman (1987) and Pope and Vetter (1989) offer discussions and empirical data on the prevalence of sexual activity between therapist and client; Gartrell (1987), Herman (1987), and Pope, Tabachnick and Keith-Spiegel (1988) examine the attitudes of mental health professionals toward this activity. As the data suggests, therapists who do not engage in such relationships are often aware of colleagues who do, however, few actually report the misconduct (Gartrell, 1987). Hence, another important area for training to address is the responsibility of colleagues for reporting such conduct or for intervening when colleagues are impaired. Brown (1990) explores this issue and the consequences of failing to do so. Corey et al. (1993), Hall (1987), Keith-Spiegel and Koocher (1985) and Lerman (1990) provide generous offerings of case studies which are useful in developing class discussions as well as written case analysis assignments.

Training must communicate that the ultimate responsibility for maintaining the boundaries of therapy rests with the therapist, not the client. Hence it may be important to devote time to discuss those occurrences when clients initiate or seek to engage the therapist in non-therapy contacts. Inexperienced therapists often assume that if the client requests such contact that it relieves them of any responsibility for the consequences.

TRAINING EXERCISES

A range of training exercises may be helpful in actively facilitating an appreciation for the complexity of ethical dilemmas in psychotherapy. At the beginning of the course therapists in training may be presented with a range of common ethical dilemmas and invited to share strategies for resolving them. This may be done without commenting on the adequacy of the solutions themselves, but in conjunction with raising questions about how they were derived. This should be repeated with similar dilemmas at various stages of the course with a focus on sharing any changes in thinking. In a written exercise trainees may be presented with case examples and required to respond to each case from two of the following perspectives: the dissatisfied client, the therapist, a professional colleague who may be aware of the therapist's conduct, or as a member of an ethics committee convened to hear the matter. A third exercise incorporates the two previous exercises. Trainees are assigned to groups of four to five members. Each group is assigned a case for analysis in which each member must assume the role of a different party and pursue the analysis from that perspective. Each group presents its case to the class and invites class participation. The latter exercise is aimed at fostering attitudes which make consultation with peers a routine occurrence.

SUMMARY

This discussion provides a review of ethical principles which a wide range of mental health disciplines deem significant. Principles reviewed here are not all inclusive and focus essentially on issues which arise with regularity in psychotherapy practice. This should not suggest that ethical considerations in teaching, research or with special populations are less important. The reader is referred to Keith-Spiegel and Koocher (1985), Lerman and Porter (1990), Pope and Vasquez (1991) and Vesper and Brock (1991) for detailed information about a wider range of ethical considerations. Furthermore, no amount of ethical principles or rules will replace sound clinical judgement. Trainees must be cautioned that such principles are designed to serve as guidelines with the assumption that psychotherapists will behave in ways that do not misuse or exploit their power or influence, promote the general welfare of the client, and generally display respect for the rights of others.

REFERENCES

Adleman, J. (1990). Necessary risks and ethical constraints: Self monitoring on values and biases. In H. Lerman & N. Porter (Eds.), *Feminist ethics in psychotherapy* (pp. 113-122). New York: Springer.

Adleman, J., & Barrett, S.E. (1990). Overlapping relations: The importance of a feminist ethical perspective. In H. Lerman & N. Porter (Eds.), *Feminist ethics in psychotherapy* (pp. 87-91). New York: Springer.

American Association for Counseling and Development. (1988). *Ethical standards* (rev. ed.). Alexandria, VA: Author.

American Association for Marriage and Family Therapy. (1991). *AAMFT code of ethics*. Washington, DC: Author.

American Mental Health Counselors Association. (1987). *Code of ethics for mental health counselors*. Alexandria, VA: Author.

American Psychoanalytic Association. (1983). *Principles of ethics for psychoanalysts and provisions for implementation of the principles of ethics for psychoanalysts*. New York: Author.

American Psychiatric Association. (1989). *The principles of medical ethics, with annotations especially applicable to psychiatry*. Washington, DC: Author.

American Psychological Association. (1992). *Ethical principles of psychologists and code of conduct*. Washington, DC: Author.

Bednar, R., Bednar, S.C., Lambert, M.J., & Waite, D.R. (1991). *Psychotherapy with high risk clients: Legal and professional standards*. Pacific Grove, CA: Brooks/Cole.

Borys, D.S. & Pope, K.S. (1989). Dual relationships between therapists and clients: A national study of psychologists, psychiatrists, and social workers. *Professional Psychology: Research and Practice*, 20, 283-293.

Bouhoutsos, J. (1985). Therapist-client sexual involvement: A challenge for mental health professionals and educators. *American Journal of Orthopsychiatry,* 55, 177-182.

Brown, L. (1988). Harmful effects of posttermination sexual and romantic relationships between therapists and their former clients. *Psychotherapy,* 25, 249-257.

Brown, L. (1990). Confronting ethically problematic behavior in feminist therapy colleagues. In H. Lerman & N. Porter (Eds.), *Feminist ethics in psychotherapy* (pp. 147-159). New York: Springer.

Cayleff, S.E. (1986). Ethical issues in counseling gender, race and culturally distinct groups. *Journal of Counseling and Development,* 64, 345-347.

Committee on Professional Standards and Board of Professional Affairs. (1987). *General guidelines for providers of psychological services.* Washington, DC: American Psychological Association.

Conte, H., Plutchik, R., Picard, S. & Toksoz, K. (1989). Ethics in the practice of psychotherapy. *American Journal of Psychotherapy,* 43, 32-42.

Corey, G., Corey, M.S., & Callanan, P. (1993). *Issues and ethics in the helping professions* (4th ed.). Belmont, CA: Brooks/Cole.

Ethics Committee of the American Psychological Association. (1988). Trends in ethics cases, common pitfalls, and published resources. *American Psychologist,* 43, 564-572.

Feminist Therapy Institute. (1990). Feminist therapy code of ethics, 1987. In H. Lerman & N. Porter (Eds.), *Feminist ethics in psychotherapy* (pp. 37-42). New York: Springer.

Gartrell, N. (1993). Boundaries in lesbian therapy relationships. *Women & Therapy,* 12, 29-50.

Gartrell, N., Herman, J., Olarte, S., Feldstein, M., & Localio, R. (1987, April). Reporting practices of psychiatrists who knew of sexual misconduct by colleagues. *American Journal of Orthopsychiatry,* 57, 287-295.

Gartrell, N., Herman, J., Olarte, S., Feldstein, M., & Localio, R. (1986). Psychiatrist-patient sexual contact: Results of a national survey, I: Prevalence. *American Journal of Psychiatry,* 143, 1126-1131.

Hall, J.E. (1987). Gender related ethical dilemmas and ethics education. *Professional Psychology: Research & Practice,* 18, 573-579.

Herman, J., Gartrell, N., Olarte, S., Feldstein, M., & Localio, R. (1987). Psychiatrist-patient sexual contact: Results of a national survey, II: Psychiatrists' attitudes. *American Journal of Psychiatry,* 144, 164-169.

Howard, D. (1990). Competence and professional self evaluation. In H. Lerman & N. Porter (Eds.), *Feminist ethics in psychotherapy* (pp. 131-136). New York: Springer.

Ibrahim, F.A., & Arredondo, P.M. (1986). Ethical standards for cross-cultural counseling: Counselor preparation, practice, assessment, and research. *Journal of Counseling and Development,* 64, 349-352.

Keith-Spiegel, P. & Koocher, G. (1985). *Ethics in psychology: Professional standards and cases.* New York: Random House.

Kentsmith, D.K., Salladay, S.A., & Miya, P.A. (Eds.). (1986). *Ethics in mental health practice.* New York: Grune & Stratton.

Kitchner, K.S. (1988). Dual role relationships: What makes them so problematic? *Journal of Counseling and Development*, 67, 217-221.

Lakin, M. (1991). *Coping with ethical dilemmas in psychotherapy.* New York: Pergamon Press.

Lerman, H. (1990). *Sexual intimacies between psychotherapists and patients: An annotated bibliography of mental health, legal and public media literature and relevant legal cases, 2nd. Ed.* Phoenix, AZ: Division of Psychotherapy, American Psychological Association.

Lerman, H., & Porter, N. (Eds.). (1990). The contribution of feminism to ethics in psychotherapy. In H. Lerman & N. Porter (Eds.), *Feminist ethics in psychotherapy* (pp. 5-13). New York: Springer.

Lerman, H. & Rigby, D. (1990). Boundary violations: Misuse of the power of the therapist. In H. Lerman & N. Porter (Eds.), *Feminist ethics in psychotherapy* (pp. 51-59). New York: Springer.

National Association of Social Workers. (1989). Standards for the private practice of clinical social work. Washington, DC: Author.

National Association of Social Workers. (1990). Code of ethics (rev. ed.). Silver Springs, MD: Author.

Pedersen, P., & Marsella, A.J. (1982). Ethical crisis for cross cultural counseling and therapy. *Professional Psychology*, 13, 492-496.

Pope, K. (1991). Dual relationships in psychotherapy. *Ethics & Behavior*, 1, 21-34.

Pope, K. & Bajt, T.R. (1988). When laws and values conflict: A dilemma for psychologists. *American Psychologist*, 43, 828-829.

Pope, K., Tabachnick, B.G., & Keith-Spiegel, P. (1988). Good and poor practices in psychotherapy: A national survey of the beliefs of psychologists. *Professional Psychology: Research and Practice*, 19, 547-552.

Pope, K., & Vasquez, M.J.T. (1991). *Ethics in psychotherapy and counseling: A practical guide for psychologists.* San Francisco, CA: Jossey Bass.

Pope, K., & Vetter, V. (1991). Prior therapist-patient sexual involvement among patients seen by psychologists. *Psychotherapy*, 28, 429-438.

Shopland, S.N., & VandeCreek, L. (1991). Sex with ex-clients: Theoretical rationales for prohibition. *Ethics & Behavior*, 1, 35-44.

Sonne, J., Meyer, C.B., Borys, D., & Marshall, V. (1985). Client's reactions to sexual intimacy in therapy. *American Journal of Orthopsychiatry*, 55, 183-189.

Tarasoff v. Regents of the University of California (1976). 17 Cal. 3d 425, 551 P.d 334.

Thompson, A. (1990). *Guide to ethical practice in psychotherapy.* New York: John Wiley & Sons.

Vasquez, M. (1991). Sexual intimacies with clients after termination: Should a prohibition be explicit? *Ethics & Behavior*, 1, 45-61.

Vesper, J.H. & Brock, G.W. (1991). *Ethics, legalities and professional practice: Issues in marital and family therapy.* Boston: Allyn & Bacon.

Zuckerman, E.L. & Guyett, I.P.R. (1991). *The paper office: Forms, guidelines and resources.* Pittsburgh, PA: Three Wishes Press.

Boundaries in Feminist Therapy:
A Conceptual Formulation

Laura S. Brown

INTRODUCTION

The attention to boundaries and boundary violations as a focus of feminist therapy work on ethics is a very persistent one. Yet as Margolies (1990) has noted, a problem for feminist therapists has been that we lack a defined, universal frame for therapy, with a related lack of clearly agreed-upon boundaries for the practice of feminist therapists. What has happened, instead, is that various authors (including myself) have attempted to develop sets of relatively concrete rules for the maintenance of boundaries in feminist therapy.

Such a concrete approach has been less than helpful, however. Rather than achieving its desired ends, e.g., to create working norms which reflect the realities of feminist therapy practice, this approach to the problem of boundaries has led prematurely to new hard and fast rules whose origins in feminist therapy precepts are

---

Laura S. Brown, PhD, ABPP, is a clinical psychologist in the independent practice of feminist psychotherapy and feminist forensic psychology in Seattle, WA, and Clinical Professor of Psychology, University of Washington. She has written extensively on the topics of ethics and boundaries in feminist therapy, and teaches workshops and does consultations on this topic, as well as other issues in feminist therapy theory.

Correspondence may be addressed to Dr. Brown at 4527 First Avenue NE, Seattle, WA 98105-4801.

[Haworth co-indexing entry note]: "Boundaries in Feminist Therapy: A Conceptual Formulation." Brown, Laura S. Co-published simultaneously in *Women & Therapy* (The Haworth Press, Inc.) Vol. 15, No. 1, 1994, pp. 29-38; and *Bringing Ethics Alive: Feminist Ethics in Psychotherapy Practice* (ed: Nanette K. Gartrell) The Haworth Press, Inc., 1994, pp. 29-38. Multiple copies of this article/chapter may be purchased from The Haworth Document Delivery Center [1-800-3-HAWORTH; 9:00 a.m. - 5:00 p.m. (EST)].

29

unclear, and which often do not reflect the contexts in which some feminist therapists practice. The closure of the discourse that ensues serves to anoint feminist "experts" on boundary issues, but leaves unresolved the alive and embodied questions of daily feminist therapy practice, particularly around perennially troublesome issues such as touch, self-disclosure, barter, and relationship overlap in which specific appropriate behaviors for every situation can be difficult to elucidate.

In the past several years, as I have been teaching workshops about boundary issues in feminist therapy in my somewhat ambivalent role as an "expert," I have repeatedly encountered this problematic trend in the form of questions that workshop participants pose to me regarding the ethical admissibility of certain specific behaviors. For example, "is it *ever* okay to hug a client?" Or, "is barter *ever* acceptable?" Or, "can you *ever* be friends with a client after therapy?" Or, "is it okay to take your shirt off at a women's music festival if your clients are there?" What I have found, to my dismay, is that when I have shared strategies that evolved into solutions that work for me, carefully framing as *my* solutions and opinions rather than "the rule," I find myself quoted two journal articles later as saying that "such and so behavior is not okay."

This is not a desirable outcome for a feminist therapy discourse on boundaries (nor do I have any great interest in being made into the authoritative source in this manner). Such premature bestowal of ultimate authority reflects the strong dominant culture norm, with which most of us struggle continuously throughout our work as feminist therapists, to anoint an expert and create a hierarchy of authority in which one woman is defined as knowledgeable, and others are constructed as either ignorant or seekers. Additionally, these questions, and the responses that have arisen to my answers reflect certain mythologies about boundaries which also can be found in dominant culture writings about this topic, myths which feminist therapists must dispel in order to continue our discourse on this question.

One myth is that of the universal frame for psychotherapy, with concomitant universal boundaries. Langs (1978) has written most extensively about this topic, propounding a very tight, neutral and abstinent frame for therapy. While it is useful to read his work as a means of understanding how he *thinks* about boundaries and their function in the therapeutic relationship, his writings betray the dominant patriarchal tendency to believe that his perspective is the correct perspective, and that there is one appropriate, non-invasive approach to creation of boundaries in psychotherapy.

The reality, which is grounded in a feminist perspective which acknowledges the diversity of human experience, is that the definition of boundaries is highly variable and reflects the factors that feminist therapists take into account in most other decision-making situations. That is, appropriate boundaries in therapy are a reflection of race, class, culture, setting, and most importantly, the specific and unique relational matrix among and between the human beings in the therapy room. A boundary which will work and facilitate treatment with one person may, because of these and other factors, be experienced as engulfing and invasive with another, or cold and punitive with a third.

A second myth which is reflected in current feminist therapy discourse on boundaries is that we can know a boundary violation when we see one, e.g., that such actions are overt and contained entirely in the behavior of the therapist. Thus, rules are promulgated for therapist behavior which assume that if certain actions are proscribed, then boundaries will be protected.

This may be true for some kinds of highly abusive behaviors such as sex with clients. However, the experience of boundary invasion tends to be an intensely private one within the phenomenology of a given client, often a response to very subtle cues which vary widely from person to person. As an example, with one woman with whom I work, it is possible for me inadvertently to time my interpretations in such a way that she will experience an invasion of her boundaries. She feels intensely interrupted, her sense of self engulfed. Another client experienced my suggestion to read a book on her issue in therapy as invasive; she felt that this suggestion was a veiled command to live her life according to various exercises in the book, and became confused when I did not understand that I had assigned her an inflexible set of rules to live by. In each of these examples, I had failed to attend to certain factors regarding what constituted boundaries for these women, having to do with their developmental issues and the symbolic nature of our relationship.

Is the point never to interrupt a client, or never to recommend a book? No; it is instead to illustrate the futility of trying to identify (and then avoid) all behaviors which are potentially boundary-violating. Making interpretations and suggesting books for clients to read are often useful, non-invasive and appropriate interventions *with some people some of the time*. It would be foolish for me, or anyone, to promulgate a rule saying "thou shalt not interrupt thy clients," or "recommend no books." But I have discovered that a risk in my sharing such illustrations in workshops is that some listeners have tended to convert them into universal rules, reflecting the mythology of how boundary violations can be identified.

A final myth regarding boundaries is that it is possible to never violate them if you follow the mythological universal rules. While this may be true for extremely egregious behaviors, the examples above illustrate that it is usually impossible to practice in such a way as never to invade our clients' sense of self or personhood because the nature of boundaries is so variable across the variety of person-situation combinations. I have earlier (Brown, 1988) discussed the notion of a continuum of boundary violation, and proposed that every therapist will move within that continuum during her time in practice based upon a number of risk factors and personal situational variables. What I would like to propose today is that a way to reduce risks for boundary violations does not lie in the identification of concrete rules regarding boundaries. Rather, it rests in our ability to understand the characteristics of a boundary violation and then to learn to ask if those characteristics are, or are highly likely to be, present in a particular instance.

CHARACTERISTICS OF BOUNDARY VIOLATIONS

I would like to describe three characteristics which I believe define violations of boundaries, and which are likely to be present to a greater or lesser degree in most situations in which a client has felt a boundary to be violated. I wish to underscore in preface that I see the client as an important source of authority on whether boundary violations have occurred; however, because so many of the people with whom we work have had their boundaries violated repeatedly and may still be struggling to know where their boundaries lie, I believe it is risky to make clients the sole source of authority on this topic, and want to emphasize that this is territory for which therapists carry the responsibility. (For example, many clients whose therapists have had sex with them had no sense that their boundaries were being violated. For the therapist to then claim, as is often the case, that the behavior is acceptable because the client did not feel violated at the time is a distortion of the feminist principal of authorizing the expertise of the client.) However, the feedback we receive from our clients about their experience of our behavior is often a valuable clue regarding when and whether we have behaved invasively in the ambiguous situations that constitute most of the challenges to ethical feminist therapy practice.

The first such characteristic of boundary violations is that they are an objectification of the client. By this I mean that the client becomes primarily an object for the satisfaction of certain needs and desires on the part of the therapist. These are usually by and of themselves acceptable needs, such as those for power, recognition, affection, and intimacy. However if these needs are met in this manner, they are likely to be destructive to the client and the psychotherapeutic relationship process. While the feminist discourse on objectification has primarily focussed on sexual objectification, I would like to suggest that there are many ways in which a client can be objectified.

For example, a client can become an object of entertainment. Each of us has probably had the experience of looking forward to our session with a particular client because we always find that person so amusing and entertaining. If this appreciation for the client's natural comedic gifts moves into a subtle encouragement that the client spend the session keeping us amused at the expense of doing their work, we have slipped into the objectification of that person. They have become important as a source of gratification for us in a way that invades or engulfs their personhood, and denies them the freedom to become un-funny because it puts their value for us at risk.

Or a client may become an educational object, an important source of information. The risks for this occurring are especially high when the client comes from a group other than our own. As I have commented earlier regarding racism in feminist therapy (Brown, 1991), such educational objectification often takes the form of a distortion of the notion of client as expert in which the client is required to teach the therapist about her/his culture in order to receive something resembling appropriate therapy. It is normal and usual for us to be informed and to learn from our clients. But the difference between that, and the transformation of the client into one whose value lies in her ability to educate us, defines the point at which a violation of boundaries may be occurring.

Emotional role reversals, as discussed by Marcia Hill (1990) are another concrete example of the general principal of objectification of a client. As Hill points out, such objectification can be brief, or can become a constant factor of the therapy relationship. The question of self-disclosure falls within this purview (Brown & Walker, 1990). It is not *whether* to self-disclose which constitutes the issue, but rather the meaning of the exchange within the relationship which ought to be our concern. It is essential to attend to the dynamics of the interchange rather than to the concrete content per se, to the meaning that it holds within this particular therapy relationship for this client and this therapist. When the effect of the encounter is to objectify the client, then the therapist's behavior may be problematic even though the same words, set in a context of different dynamics and intentions, might not be violating in that second instance.

A second characteristic of boundary violations is that they are an acting out or gratification of the therapist's impulses. Such impulses can be quite benign, and appear caring and nurturing; or, they may be expressions of important confrontation. Yet because they are impulsive, that is, not carefully thought through and assessed as to their specific effect on the client and the therapy relationship, they carry the risk of invading or engulfing the client rather than assisting the process of psychotherapeutic change.

For instance, the impulse to hug a client. We are dealing here with the impulse for the behavior, not the behavior itself (this is an important distinction which tends to get lost in most discussions of boundary issues). If I act impulsively, then I am indulging my own needs, whatever they might be; to be comforting, to quiet the crying client, to establish a sense of contact. Whatever those impulses might be, and however loving, they are self-centered in a way that fails to take into account who the client is, and how they will receive our impulsive behavior.

For example, a therapist began to hug and hold her client whenever the latter, a survivor of multiple sexual abuse by both male and female care-givers, became tearful and regressed in therapy sessions. The therapist became very confused when the client began to complain that she, the client, was feeling sexually abused by the therapist, and sexually aroused by the nurturing holding. The therapist had, in her impulsivity, failed to take into account how the client would receive and experience this touch which was clearly intended in a nurturing and non-sexual manner. As this illustration delineates, impulsivity on the part of the therapist ignores the relational and interpersonal as well as symbolic components of our behavior. In this particular case the enactment of the therapist's nurturing impulses had very painful and frightening consequences for the client, as well as for the therapist, who had great difficulty coping with an image of herself as a sexually abusive person.

Again, this is *not* to proscribe the nurturing holding of clients per se. Rather, it is to point out that it is the nature of the transaction, in this case the impulsivity and lack of diagnostic clarity with which an intervention is delivered, which constitutes its underlying potential to be invasive or engulfing. It is important for us, as feminist therapists, to ask ourselves how we have arrived at the decision to engage in a certain behavior, and whether or not our actions are impulsive rather than understood. Our sources of information in moving away from impulsivity may, in fact, be non-rational ones; intuition, unconscious information in the form of dreams, images, or music in the mind are equally good ways of knowing as are more rational, conscious ones. Impulsivity is not the same as acting from intuitive knowing, because the latter is considered and integrated into the whole of therapy, while the former is simply done because it feels good to the therapist in the moment.

A final characteristic of boundary violations that I would like to propose here is that they place the needs of the therapist paramount in a consistent and persistent manner. The place of the therapist's needs in therapy is controversial and problematic; if our work were not need-gratifying in some manner, we would no doubt cease to do it. Often the non-conscious motivations behind our choice of therapy as a career lead to a sense of frustration or dissatisfaction, even burnout, because of the difficulties inherent in meeting certain normative human needs in the role of psychotherapist.

There are also certain needs of the therapist which may be important to have met within the frame of therapy as a given. For instance, our need for control over time, and for income, are among those which are subsumed into such common therapy practices as the 50-minute hour and the requirement of payment for services rendered in most cases. Additionally, many of us will have important human needs met inadvertently and unintentionally in our work as therapists; we will have the honor of experiencing a form of intimacy, of feeling loved and admired, of being valued and cherished simply because we are present, doing what we do.

Where this all becomes confusing, and where potential distortions of the process can occur and lead to boundary violations, is in the overlap between relationships in general, and the specific psychotherapeutic relationship. In non-therapy relationships, it is quite natural that at times, and often for extended periods of time, our needs, whatever they may be, are the most important ones in the relationship. In the dance of relationships, many of us enter the work of therapy quite skilled at being children, parents, partners, teachers; each a dance with its own steps and rhythm, each with steps which will be similar to those of the dance of therapy. Yet a step in those dances which cannot be present when we are therapist is that of the solo performer, the center of attention. Therapy is always a pas de deux in which we are the supporting partner.

When we forget which dance we are dancing, or mistake the dance of therapy for all others that we do, no matter how well, then our own needs can become the most important ones in the equation, choreographed into the relationship in ways which will diminish the centrality of the client. The client who we ask for a ride to pick up our car from the mechanic is being asked to make our need for the ride paramount, no less so than the client being asked to have sex with us. Depending on the person who receives the request, the potential for harm in asking such a modest favor can be great indeed.

As these three characteristics illustrate, a central theme running through this process of understanding boundary violations is that they often occur when the *relational* nature of therapy is forgotten, and work begins to center around the self and person of the therapist. The emergence of this theme underscores the importance for therapists, feminist and otherwise, to create opportunities to do the purely human things in our lives outside of our work–objectification, impulsivity, self-centeredness–ways of being that in therapy, with its unequal balance of power and complex conscious and non-conscious symbolic dynamics, would be considered boundary violations.

CONCLUSION

When a feminist therapist begins to apply this conceptual framework to the question of boundaries in psychotherapy, confusion will almost always be the first outcome. This is because no clear rules will immediately emerge about which behaviors constitute a boundary violation. But that is precisely the goal of this method. In order to utilize a conceptual rather than a concrete model for defining boundary violations, a therapist must continuously be thinking, feeling, and making sense of situations as they arise.

For some therapists, this process will lead to personal guidelines that are useful. This has been my experience; as I come to know what interpersonal configurations and internal processes are likely to bring me into one or some combination of all three of these boundary-violating ways of being, I have developed for myself examples of what works in general, and what does not. I have also had underscored for me how each new client brings with her the requirement that I understand in a careful and diagnostic manner what will violate her, and how and to what degree she is able to know and communicate about such invasions or engulfments.

This method creates the requirement and possibility that our process of understanding boundaries in feminist therapy includes the input of the people with whom we work. In keeping with the feminist ethic of empowerment, our willingness to attend carefully to what we are told about what creates distress, and to incorporate that into our therapeutic relationship with a client means that we support and reward clients for reclaiming the power to know who they are, and where their edges are. This is a process that no concrete rules can ever encompass, because such a methodology assumes that we, as therapists and rule-promulgators, are always the only experts. Utilizing a conceptual framework such as the one proposed here makes the process of maintaining boundaries in therapy a shared, powerful, and empowering experience.

It is likely that boundary violations have other characteristics than the ones that I have identified (and I look forward greatly to the input of readers and suggestions regarding other concepts for exploration). My hope is that in proposing these three, I have framed the discourse in a manner which will move increasingly away from the concrete and into strategies which will allow each feminist therapist to claim her own expertise regarding boundaries in psychotherapy.

NOTE

As always, my work arises from interactions with others. I would especially like to thank the staff of the WCREC in Toronto Ontario and the participants at workshops I presented at Feminist Counseling Associates in Vancouver BC for the opportunity to do some of the work in progress on this piece. My thanks also to several clients whose feedback to me has been essential in understanding the importance of thinking diagnostically about boundary violations.

REFERENCES

Brown, L.S. (1988). Beyond thou shalt not: Thinking about ethics in the lesbian therapy community. *Women & Therapy*, 8, 13-26.
Brown, L.S. (1991). Anti-racism as an ethical imperative: An example from feminist therapy. *Ethics and Behavior*, 1, 113-127.
Brown, L.S. & Walker, L.E.A. (1990). Feminist therapy perspectives on self-disclosure. In G. Stricker & M. Fisher (Eds.), *Self-disclosure in the therapeutic relationship* (pp. 135-156). New York: Plenum.
Hill, M. (1990). On creating a theory of feminist therapy. In L.S. Brown & M.P.P. Root (Eds.). *Diversity and complexity in feminist therapy.* (pp. 53-66). New York: The Haworth Press, Inc.
Langs, R. (1978). *The listening process.* New York: Jason Aronson.
Margolies, L. (1990). Cracks in the frame: Feminism and the boundaries of therapy. *Women & Therapy*, 9, 19-36.

Sexual Abuse
of Women by Women in Psychotherapy:
Counseling and Advocacy

Nanette K. Gartrell
Barbara E. Sanderson

INTRODUCTION

In most mental health settings, the relationship between caregiver and client is a crucial tool in the healing process. Because clients

---

Nanette K. Gartrell, MD, is Associate Clinical Professor of Psychiatry at the University of California, San Francisco, where she teaches ethics and feminist therapy theory. She has a private psychotherapy practice in San Francisco. Barbara Sanderson, MA, is Director, Ethics in Practice, a consulting firm in Minnetonka, MN. She is former coordinator of the Minnesota State Task Force on Sexual Exploitation by Counselors and Therapists.

Correspondence may be addressed to Dr. Gartrell at 3570 Clay Street, San Francisco, CA 94118.

[Haworth co-indexing entry note]: "Sexual Abuse of Women by Women in Psychotherapy: Counseling and Advocacy." Gartrell, Nanette K., and Barbara E. Sanderson. Co-published simultaneously in *Women & Therapy* (The Haworth Press, Inc.) Vol. 15, No. 1, 1994, pp. 39-54; and *Bringing Ethics Alive: Feminist Ethics in Psychotherapy Practice* (ed: Nanette K. Gartrell) The Haworth Press, Inc., 1994, pp. 39-54. Multiple copies of this article/chapter may be purchased from The Haworth Document Delivery Center [1-800-3-HAWORTH; 9:00 a.m. - 5:00 p.m. (EST)].

39

typically seek treatment at times of emotional duress, both their own pain and the process of requesting help from a professional place them in a highly vulnerable position. The relationship is one-way, in that the client is neither privileged to personal information about her caregiver, nor is she expected to provide reciprocal assistance to the caregiver. Consequently, such relationships are always unequal, and the power resides with the caregiver. Professional skill and discipline are required to utilize this power constructively. If the caregiver lacks skill or personal insight, this power may be mismanaged in a way that is hurtful to clients. Clients may also be hurt intentionally, through conscious manipulation. Regardless of whether sex between counselor and client occurs because of inadequate training or conscious manipulation, it is never acceptable professional behavior.

There is an extensive literature on the effect of male therapist-female client abuse on clients. To some extent, this reflects the gender distribution in reported cases: 80% involve male therapists and female clients, 13% are female-female, 5% are male-male, and 2% involve female therapists and male clients (Schoener, Milgrom, Gonsiorek, Luepker, & Conroe, 1989). Relatively little has been written about female-female abuse, even though some aspects of same-gender abuse can contribute to a particularly difficult recovery for the victim. For example, if a client selects a female or lesbian therapist because she feels more trusting of women or lesbians, and that therapist later exploits her, the client may feel doubly betrayed. The client may also feel as though she has no remaining options for mental health care, since she now perceives both male and female providers as unsafe.

The relative paucity of literature on female-female abuse has multiple determinants. It may reflect a wish on the part of some feminist therapists to deny the power differential between therapists and clients. Even though some of the involved therapists consider themselves heterosexual, same-gender abuse stigmatizes the lesbian community, and most of us prefer to avoid highlighting any conduct which might have that outcome. Also, many of us who are considered pioneers in this field have focused our efforts on clarifying ethics codes, establishing legal statutes, and educating our colleagues, in the hope that we might decrease the prevalence of this particularly devastating type of abuse. Unfortunately, however, these efforts have sometimes allowed us to overlook the problems which have occurred in our own backyards.

Not surprisingly, women who expose abuse by feminist and/or lesbian therapists sometimes have difficulty garnering support for their efforts. One can ascribe this lack of support, in part, to the fact that feminist and lesbian institutions are often founded out of a desire for alternatives to the sexism and homophobia of our culture. Acknowledging that abuse can exist in our institutions is painful for us because it implies that no absolutely safe place exists for women. We are particularly reluctant to confront prominent women whose conduct has been exploitative. Placing such women above censure denies them the opportunity to receive constructive feedback. A hierarchy is created in which prominent women are not expected to behave ethically—a situation which, ironically, replicates the white, male, heterosexist institutions from which many of us originally sought refuge. Exempting our leaders from ethical conduct is sometimes justified by claims that their contributions will outweigh any damage they may cause. When sexual exploitation is ignored within a system, however, tolerance for abuse increases until it becomes the norm.

The view that men are dangerous and that women are not can create a temporary illusion of safety; however, another view of human behavior is necessary to prevent sexual exploitation and to deal successfully with its aftermath. Everyone has weaknesses, which can be exacerbated in times of exceptional stress. Given the right set of circumstances, any mental health professional could become abusive (Stefanson, 1985). We are most likely to get into serious difficulty if people around us do not hold us accountable for our actions.

Women can help to counteract the destructive power of sexual abuse within our institutions by making it publicly clear that we expect ethical behavior from all women and that we will hold each other accountable for abuse. We also can reward, rather than punish, those women who take responsible action and speak out about abuse. If we conceal abuse in the mistaken belief that we are protecting the organizations and communities we have worked so hard to establish, we demonstrate our own internalized sexism and homophobia. The end result is that we lower our standards to expect less of ourselves than we do of men.

In the following case studies, we will examine the difficult challenges created for colleagues of exploitative women mental health professionals. One of us (N.G. or B.S.) consulted on each case. All cases have been disguised to protect confidentiality.

The case sequence represents the continuum of abusive professional behavior described by Schoener and Gonsiorek (1989). In the first case, a gradual deterioration of boundaries between psychiatrist and client resulted in sexual exploitation. The second case illustrates how insufficient training and internalized homophobia contributed to client abuse. In the third case, the caregiver denied her counseling role in a series of exploitative relationships with counselees. The therapist in the fourth case manipulated both clients and staff and became sexually involved with several clients during the same period. Additionally, Cases II through IV illustrate some of the ways that counseling and advocacy organizations can be tainted by sexual exploitation.

CASE I. PRIVATE PRACTICE PSYCHIATRIST

A 53-year-old married woman psychiatrist was treating a 35-year-old heterosexual client (Ms. A). Ms. A was an incest survivor who had entered treatment because of her inability to find a meaningful relationship. Over time the psychiatrist developed a deep attachment to her. The psychiatrist did not seek supervision or consultation on this case. During the fourth month of treatment, she began to see Ms. A late in the day for two- to three-hour sessions, for which Ms. A was not billed. As Ms. A began working through her incest memories, she became increasingly depressed, and the psychiatrist began holding and caressing her during sessions. The psychiatrist also prescribed antidepressant medication.

During the sixth month of treatment, the psychiatrist separated from her husband of eight years. When Ms. A was forced to move by a substantial rent increase, the psychiatrist suggested that the client move into an apartment over her garage. They became sexually involved several weeks later.

The psychiatrist soon began identifying herself as a lesbian.

Eager to make contact with other lesbian therapists, she came out to a number of therapists in her community. When she acknowledged her involvement with Ms. A, some associates–both lesbian and heterosexual–quietly withdrew from collegial relationships with her. These therapists neither confronted the psychiatrist nor notified her professional association or licensing board.

Two years later the relationship between the psychiatrist and Ms. A began to deteriorate. Ms. A returned home to find that the locks had been changed. A note on the front door indicated that all her belongings had been moved into a storage facility. She left numerous messages on the psychiatrist's answering machine, but the psychiatrist never returned her calls. Ms. A became suicidally depressed. She was admitted to an inpatient psychiatric unit after overdosing on her antidepressant medication. She continued to hold on to the fantasy that she and the psychiatrist would eventually be reunited, and she never disclosed the reason for her depression during her two-month hospitalization. The psychiatrist is still in private practice.

This is a case in which progressive dissolution of boundaries resulted in sexual exploitation of a client. The first indication of a potential problem came when the psychiatrist failed to seek consultation as her feelings toward Ms. A intensified. Instead, she began to act out her feelings by loosening boundaries: offering longer sessions, meeting late in the day, and discontinuing billing. In addition, she ignored the fact that incest survivors may have a particularly difficult time setting limits on touch (Brown, 1989) as she began holding and caressing Ms. A.

The psychiatrist then came out to other therapists in her community. Those therapists who identified the situation as abusive quietly withdrew–without confronting her or notifying her licensing board. Their response is consistent with Gartrell et al.'s findings on psychiatrists who know offenders: only 6% file complaints against their colleagues (Gartrell, Herman, Olarte, Feldstein, & Localio, 1987). Since 33-80% of offending therapists have been sexual with more than one client (Gartrell, Herman, Olarte, Feldstein, & Localio, 1987; Pope, 1979), colleagues who collude by their silence are not only preventing a current victim from receiving the immediate assistance she needs, but also are endangering the future clients of a known offender.

CASE II. CHURCH: COUNSELING CLERGY

In recent years, a traditional denomination began ordaining women ministers. Despite having a sizeable gay/lesbian constituency, the denominational leaders refused to allow ordination of gays or lesbians. A newly-ordained woman was hired as assistant pastor in a large, urban church with a very progressive gay/lesbian outreach program. Soon after she arrived, she began providing marital counseling for a mother of three in her congregation who had been physically abused by her husband. Like most clergy who provide counseling services, she had no counseling training and no supervision.

The assistant pastor became very involved in helping the mother leave her husband and retain custody of the children. Because her husband had not allowed her to have friends, she had no support other than the assistant pastor. The two women developed a deep attachment to each other, which eventually led to a sexual relationship. They were extremely closeted about their relationship.

The assistant pastor consistently denied being a lesbian. When the mother pushed her to come out, the pastor became very resistant until the relationship eventually ended. The mother turned to a lesbian member of the congregation in her grief at the loss of the relationship. This woman reported the assistant pastor to the other ministers of the church. These ministers experienced considerable conflict over the alleged abuse. Some expressed fear and anger about the potential threat to their controversial outreach program. Others advocated informing the governing board, so that disciplinary action could be taken against the assistant pastor. Several ministers argued that such an action would make it even less likely that gays and lesbians would be ordained in the future. When they contacted the mother, she made it quite clear that she did not want to take any action, because she did not feel that the assistant pastor had done anything wrong.

Ultimately the ministers decided that the mother would be revictimized if her wishes were not respected. The church counsel advised against reprimanding the assistant pastor since the mother was unwilling to file a complaint. Therefore, the ministers pursued their only remaining option–hiring consultants to educate the congrega-

tion about sexual misconduct by clergy. They are also urging the national denomination to adopt clear-cut policies on appropriate boundaries between clergy and congregants. The offending assistant pastor is being closely supervised to prevent further abuse. She is now only allowed to make referrals to counseling services, rather than providing services for which she is not trained.

Internalized homophobia often results in an individual's refusal to identify herself as lesbian. This denial may make a caregiver more vulnerable to acting out with clients (Gonsiorek, 1989). The problem is exacerbated when organizational policy forces lesbians to be closeted. In this denomination, as in most others, lesbians must choose between an open lifestyle and ordination. Any situation that necessitates the keeping of a secret is fertile ground for exploitation (White, 1986).

In this case well-intentioned support for an abused constituent led to a sexual relationship which had potential consequences for the entire denomination. Individuals who were directly or potentially harmed by the assistant pastor's conduct included:

1. The mother who experienced increased vulnerability and additional loss.
2. Other women ministers and women seeking ordination, since the assistant pastor was one of the first women to be ordained in the denomination.
3. Other lesbian/gay congregants whose controversial outreach program may be threatened.
4. Gays and lesbians hoping to be ordained in the denomination, whose ordination may be further delayed.
5. The other ministers who had to live with the knowledge that they could not take direct action against an abusive colleague.

Colleagues of a known offender face a particularly difficult dilemma when the victim does not want to file a complaint. Even though it may be painful for organizations or individuals to pass up the opportunity to confront a perpetrator, it is usually wise to leave the decision in the hands of the victim. To do otherwise runs the risk of mimicking the abusive situation by taking control away from the victim. Those who continue to feel frustrated by the victim's choice may benefit from organizing educational programs on abuse. Such activities can counteract feelings of helplessness which occur when it is not possible to take punitive action against a known offender.

CASE III. BATTERED WOMEN'S SHELTER/SEXUAL ASSAULT CENTER: PAID AND VOLUNTEER STAFF

The founding mother (Ms. B) of a combination battered women's shelter/sexual assault center was a woman who had been severely abused by her husband before she came out as a lesbian. She was neither trained nor licensed as a therapist. In fact, she had a strong aversion to psychotherapy because she had found it so unhelpful during her attempts to leave her husband. She felt that her therapist had blamed her for her husband's abuse, and had discouraged her from leaving.

Ms. B had lobbied long and hard with the state legislature to provide funding for the center. Although she and most of the center's staff were lesbians, they were publicly closeted because of their concern about homophobia affecting funding. Through Ms. B's dedication and effort, the center grew from an all-volunteer staff to a staff that was 75% paid and 25% volunteer. Ms. B essentially lived at the center, and considered the staff and clients her "family." Many clients eventually became volunteers at the center, and some joined the permanent staff. Sexual involvement among staff members was common.

Clients typically came to the center for crisis intervention after sexual assault or battery, or with new memories of earlier sexual abuse. Hugging was considered part of the healing process for clients, and hugs were dispensed liberally by the staff. Clients were not encouraged to make their own decisions about hugging, and the staff did not make it a practice to inquire what the hugs meant to individual clients. Clients were also actively discouraged from seeking psychotherapy; the staff claimed that it was disruptive to the healing process. Also, the staff did not believe in making diagnostic distinctions among clients because the center's overall policy was that "we are all the same." Therefore, clients who were more vulnerable due to a history of mental illness were not referred for follow-up mental health treatment.

Ms. C first came to the center after being raped. Later she joined the staff as a volunteer. During her volunteer training, Ms. C became aware of the fact that she had been sexually abused by her step-father. Ms. B began meeting with Ms. C privately to discuss these issues. Ms. C felt very grateful to have these meetings which she considered "counseling sessions." Ms. B held and stroked her frequently during these sessions, and eventually the contact became sexual. Ms. B repeatedly said that "healing physical contact" was what Ms. C "needed." Ms. B insisted that the sexual contact be kept secret, because she was worried about losing funding for the center if she were identified as a lesbian. Ms. C discovered through friends that two other clients had also had sexual relationships with Ms. B while working on their memories of childhood sexual abuse. Both women said they loved and trusted Ms. B. Neither saw any reason to complain about her behavior. Nevertheless, Ms. C began to feel exploited. When Ms. C. confronted Ms. B about her conduct, Ms. B said that she had a special ability to help incest victims and would do anything in her power to help them. When Ms. C began to tell her colleagues at the center about being sexually exploited by Ms. B, she was soundly criticized, and eventually ostracized from the statewide sexual assault/battered women's community.

Although Ms. B had dedicated her life to providing services for abused and battered women, the center she established perpetuated many of the boundary violations its clients were seeking to escape. Defining all psychotherapists as unhelpful denied clients the opportunity to learn strategies which may have enabled them to become less vulnerable. Women with major mental illness were discouraged from seeking necessary treatment. Also, by insisting that hugs were a necessary aspect of the healing process, particularly vulnerable women were not helped to set limits. Since the center's staff were neither licensed nor regulated, there was no complaint mechanism available for those whose mental health was further compromised by this unethical conduct.

In addition, Ms. B offered her services as a counselor (even though she did not call herself that) to vulnerable individuals, and then became sexually involved with at least three of them. Identifying this behavior as abusive challenged two major myths about the shelter/assault community: (1) that shelters/centers are the only safe islands in a dangerous world; and, (2) that women are never abusers. The community resistance to acknowledging Ms. B's abusive behavior highlights a double standard concerning gender. If the dominant individual had been a Mr. B rather than a Ms. B, most feminists would not hesitate to label his conduct exploitative. However, a sexual relationship between a dominant and subordinate female who were engaged in a counseling relationship was rationalized as loving, supportive, and nurturing. Such rationalizations are not uncommon when the dominant individual has made such a profound contribution to the women's community.

Some may argue that it is anti-feminist to challenge Ms. B about her abusive conduct because the shelter/assault center would never have existed without her. Whereas Ms. B should be commended for her contributions to the lives of so many women, she also deserves censure for her abusive conduct. The center's basic tenet of not respecting interpersonal boundaries should also be challenged.

Others may raise concerns about a homophobic backlash that could occur if the internal abuse were brought out into the open. Homophobia clouds the issue of same sex abuse regardless of the sexual orientation of the involved women. Because lesbians experience so much discrimination, sexual exploitation between a female professional and a female client is often confused with the right of adults to choose their own sexual partners. Sexual exploitation is *not* about freedom of association. When sexual exploitation is equated with freedom of association, it lends credibility to the homophobic notion that Homosexual = Abuser. A similar phenomenon occurs when homosexual perpetrators of child sexual abuse are defended with the argument that these acts were simply an expression of their homosexuality. In relationships with a built-in power differential, abuse is never an expression of sexual orientation. When same-sex abuse occurs, it is the perpetrator who is responsible for any homophobic backlash, not the victim/survivor, nor the colleague who brings the misconduct to light.

It is true that both state budgetary and private financial support for shelters/assault programs could be adversely affected if the abuse became public. It would be far preferable for center staff to clean house internally by bringing in consultants and establishing a training program on the dynamics of exploitation. If these internal solutions are not successful, the abuse should be brought to public attention. A less decisive strategy replicates the incestuous systems from which many victim/survivors seek protection. If exposure is considered taboo, perpetrators can be abusive without consequences. If speaking out results in ostracism by one's peers, there may be no place to turn for support. Community ostracism also discourages others from coming forward because they have witnessed the consequences.

CASE IV. FEMINIST THERAPY COLLECTIVE

In the late 1970s a feminist therapy collective was established in a city with a large and active women's community. The collective was pioneered by a very charismatic and highly-regarded lesbian clinical psychologist. In addition to the psychologist, the collective included two recent Masters of Social Work (MSW) graduates from a program where the psychologist taught, as well as an Education Doctorate (EdD) graduate student intern. During graduate school, the psychologist had been sexually involved with one of her women professors. Before establishing the collective, she had had brief sexual relationships with several of her clients. The psychologist claimed that feminist therapy was not hierarchical and that she considered clients were peers in the therapeutic relationship. She socialized freely with clients, bartered for services (including exchanging massage for psychotherapy), and occasionally loaned money to clients. She advocated sexual involvement with clients as long as both therapist and client had fully discussed their feelings prior to the involvement. She encouraged other collective members to become sexually involved with their clients; she was typically involved with several clients simultaneously. Many women who were treated by this collective had their first lesbian sexual experience when they became involved with collective members.

Ten years after its founding a new collective member (Ms. D) became alarmed when she learned of the collective's history of exploitation. She consulted a lesbian former professor. The professor encouraged Ms. D to handle the problem internally to avoid a homophobic backlash from the collective's referral sources. Before Ms. D had decided on a course of action, another of the collective's therapists was sued by a client for sexual abuse. Although the case was settled quietly out of court, the abused client informed the women's community about the collective's history of violations. At that time the collective included six full-time and three part-time therapists, all of whom had been supervised by the founding psychologist. When the collective began to be pressured by other feminist therapists and collectives to discontinue the sexual exploitation, only Ms. D and one other therapist had not had allegations of sexual exploitation made against them. Nevertheless, these two women, with the support of a skilled clinical supervisor outside the agency, were able to institute a thorough house-cleaning within the collective. The founding psychologist expressed no remorse about her conduct and moved to another state to avoid legal action and license revocation.

The remaining members established a comprehensive training program on the dynamics of exploitation. Participation in this training program was required for all new collective members. Even with this training, the old collective members struggled constantly with their basic assumptions about the therapeutic process and professional boundaries. Weekly case consultation with a supervisor skilled in these issues was required for all collective members.

The publicity regarding the exploitation brought some of the collective's abused clients back into treatment with therapists outside the collective. Despite having established long-term committed lesbian relationships (some with children conceived by alternative insemination), these clients were now expressing fears that perhaps they were not lesbians after all, since they had come out in the context of an abusive relationship. Some of those who became feminists during treatment by the collective questioned the origins of their understanding of feminism. Several of these women are considering a lawsuit against the collective to pay for their subsequent therapy to recover from the abuse. This possibility prompted the collective to locate past client victims to offer restitution and referrals. The collective's malpractice insurance carrier is threatening to cancel its policy if another suit occurs.

This collective was established by a very powerful community leader and her subordinates (two students and a trainee). It is possible that the term "collective" was not even an appropriate term for the group during the early years, since the founding psychologists's standard of *mal*practice became normative for the group. Even if the other members had disagreed with this standard, they were probably too subordinate to challenge her authority.

This case illustrates a modeling effect for sexual abuse (Pope et al., 1979): the psychologist first became sexually involved with one of her professors, then with many of her clients. Her dominant position within the collective allowed her conduct to become the standard for the group. This standard not only allowed sexual involvement with clients, but also included a nonhierarchial treatment model with loose to nonexistent boundaries and confusion about the power differential between therapists and clients. Many professionals were trained within this model before the first lawsuit occurred.

It took considerable stamina for a subordinate to challenge the founding psychologist and her allies. Even though she was backed by other therapists in the community, this kind of confrontation required fortitude and resourcefulness. The collective subsequently made a serious effort to educate members about the dynamics of exploitation. Unfortunately, this housecleaning did not prevent the founding psychologist from escaping the consequences of her abusive actions.

COMMENT

Since the relationship between counselor and client is one of the most basic and important tools in the healing process, its use and misuse are of everyday concern to mental health professionals. This article discusses the misuse of power by women counselors and therapists who sexually exploit their women clients. Although we were tempted to share our own affective responses along with a more critical analysis of each case, we chose instead to allow these cases to speak for themselves. Past experience has shown us that our own commentary stimulates reactions to us, rather than the cases. Typically we are cast in the role of authority figures who wish to restrict freedom of association. When we limit our commentary, we find that audiences are more willing to acknowledge their own positions of power, and to take responsibility for the use and misuse of power in their own professional relationships.

The cases we have presented illustrate many of the factors which contribute to a suspension of therapeutic boundaries in the name of romance. The rationalizations used by abusive female therapists which mirror those of their male counterparts include: (1) claims of mutual attraction/infatuation between counselor and client; and (2) assertions that clients are consenting adults who are fully capable of selecting their own sexual partners. In addition, some female abusers engage in the dynamic of denying or ignoring the power differential between themselves and their clients—often in the name of feminism. Accompanying this denial is the assumption that women or feminists cannot be abusive because we do not have access to patriarchal power. The fact is that all therapists—regardless of gender—are powerful in relation to clients. Therapy abuse is much more likely to occur when this power differential is denied. Other factors which set the background for a potentially abusive relationship include a prior history of abuse in the counselor and/or the client, the greater trust women clients place in female caregivers over male, and the ambiguity that sometimes arises when nurturance and caring are confused with sexuality.

This article also highlights the various difficulties and challenges for colleagues of a known offender. Colleagues must consider the options of reporting an offense and confronting the offender. Inevitably, these options are anxiety provoking—since we risk ostracization by our women's or lesbian community for speaking out, especially if the accused is one of our leaders. We also must confront our own doubts about the veracity of the claim (and our fear that someday we may be falsely accused), our lingering guilt about erotic feelings we have experienced toward some clients, and our community rumor mill which spins tales about occasional sexual relationships between women therapists and clients which allegedly work out. If the accused is a close and trusted friend or colleague, we may have considerable difficulty sorting out facts from feelings. Despite these conflicting loyalties and fears of reprisal, we are obligated as mental health professionals to protect the public from abusive colleagues. At the minimum, any accusation deserves a thorough investigation.

The protection and proper treatment of clients are as fundamental as the survival of any specific organization, and indeed may be critical to the survival (or failure) of any organization that neglects them. Several of the case studies presented in this article highlight the prominent role that individuals can play in creating a climate that is either conducive or inimicable to sexual exploitation within organizations or communities. Agencies providing counseling and advocacy services for women should establish clear guidelines so that abusive treatment of clients is not fostered or tolerated. This type of organizational policy will create a standard in women's organizations that is consistent with feminist theory. It is also important not to let our concerns about homophobia prevent us from addressing impropriety in our organizations. Indeed, one of the best protections against the intrusion of homophobia is for us to tend to our own ethical responsibilities before we are required to do so by external mandates.

In acknowledging that women caregivers can be abusive, all women must face the fact that there is no place which is absolutely safe from exploitation. However, we can increase our experience of safety in therapeutic relationships by advocating a standard of practice for women professionals that includes abstention from exploitative contact with clients. We must also hold each other accountable for exploitative conduct, and support those who refuse to keep silent about their own abuse or their abusive colleagues. We hope that this article will be a catalyst for thought and discussion toward these goals.

NOTE

The authors would like to thank the following colleagues for their assistance with this article: Joan Biren, Laura Brown, Maricia Chamberlain, Dianna Diers, Mary Eichbauer, John Gonsiorek, Marny Hall, Karen Johnson, Minnie Bruce Pratt, Gary Schoener, and Ann Stefanson.

REFERENCES

Brown, L.S. (1989). Beyond thou shalt not: Thinking about ethics in the lesbian therapy community. *Women & Therapy.* 8(1/2), 13-25.

Gartrell, N., Herman, J., Olarte, S., Feldstein, M., & Localio, R. (1987). Reporting practices of psychiatrists who knew of sexual misconduct by colleagues. *American Journal of Orthopsychiatry*, 57(2), 287-295.

Gonsiorek, J.C. (1989). Sexual exploitation by psychotherapists: Some observations on male victims and on sexual orientation concerns. In Sanderson, B.E., *It's never OK: A handbook for professionals on sexual exploitation by counselors and therapists.* St. Paul, Minnesota: Minnesota Department of Corrections.

Pope, K.S., Levenson, H., & Schover, L.R. (1979). Sexual intimacy in psychology training: Results and implications of a National survey. *American Psychologist,* 34, 682-689.

Schoener, G.R. & Gonsiorek, J.C. (1989). Assessment and development of rehabilitation plans for the therapist. In Schoener, G.R., Milgrom, J.H., Gonsiorek, J.C., Luepker, E.T., & Conroe, R.M. *Psychotherapists involvement with clients: Intervention and prevention.* Minneapolis, Minnesota: Walk-In Counseling Center.

Schoener, G.R., Milgrom, J.H., Gonsiorek, J.C., Luepker, E.T., & Conroe, R.M. (1989). *Psychotherapists' sexual involvement with clients: Intervention and prevention.* Minneapolis, Minnesota: Walk-In Counseling Center.

Stefanson, A. (1985). Countertransference issues for therapists working with sexually exploitative therapists. In: Sanderson, B.E., *It's never OK: A handbook for professionals on sexual exploitation by counselors and therapists.* St. Paul, Minnesota: Minnesota Department of Corrections.

White, L.W. (1986). *Incest in the organizational family: The ecology of burnout in closed systems.* Bloomington, Illinois: The Lighthouse Training Institute.

Therapist Sexual Misconduct

Pauline P. DeLozier

According to Caroline Heilbrun in her book *Writing A Woman's Life*, "The true representation of power is not of a big man beating a smaller man or a woman. Power is the ability to take one's place in whatever discourse is essential to action and the right to have one's part matter. This is true in the Pentagon, in marriage, in friendship, and in politics" (p. 18). It also is true for mental health practitioners.

In our profession, we have recognized our responsibility and our power to address the discourse pertaining to issues of abuse and abuse recovery. While these areas are not the exclusive concern of the psychological service professions and indeed are being addressed in many public and professional arenas, they are of central importance in the helping and healing professions. These are often the very issues brought to the therapeutic encounter, the very issues with which the client or patient needs assistance. Therefore it is critical that mental health practitioners become well grounded in knowledge about abuse issues and prepared to assist in the resolu-

Pauline P. DeLozier, PhD, is a clinical psychologist in practice in Santa Ana, CA, and has been Regional Department Head and Chief of Staff for a managed care health plan for eleven years. Dr. DeLozier's eighteen-year clinical practice and her research has focused on issues regarding abuse and recovery, and on attachment, separation and loss; she has consulted and presented both nationally and internationally in these fields.

Correspondence may be addressed to Dr. DeLozier at 21 Bluebird Lane, Aliso Viejo, CA 92656.

[Haworth co-indexing entry note]: "Therapist Sexual Misconduct." DeLozier, Pauline P. Co-published simultaneously in *Women & Therapy* (The Haworth Press, Inc.) Vol. 15, No. 1, 1994, pp. 55-67; and *Bringing Ethics Alive: Feminist Ethics in Psychotherapy Practice* (ed: Nanette K. Gartrell) The Haworth Press, Inc., 1994, pp. 55-67. Multiple copies of this article/chapter may be purchased from The Haworth Document Delivery Center [1-800-3-HAWORTH; 9:00 a.m. - 5:00 p.m. (EST)].

tion of the resulting damage, as well as able to avoid further impairment of the people they seek to help. Furthermore, from the viewpoint of feminist ethics and treatment, the use and abuse of power in any and all relationships is a primary focus of therapy. It is through the examination of past and current power imbalances or abuses and through the gradual empowerment of the client that therapeutic change takes place. It is through modeling the responsible use of power and the responsible setting and enforcing of boundaries that the clinician structures an environment conducive to positive growth.

The specific abuse issues of concern in this article are those resulting from the inability of the practitioner to maintain appropriate boundaries and to use the power differential in the therapeutic encounter in the best interest of the client, particularly when the boundary violations and inappropriate use of power involves therapist sexual misconduct. The question of subsequent treatment for clients previously violated by a clinician also warrants attention. There is a clear need to identify and address the ethical problems, to assist in recovery for affected clients, and to educate mental health practitioners in order to avoid further injury.

Recent public and professional attention has focused on therapist sexual misconduct as a critical ethical and legal dilemma in mental health service delivery. Legislative bodies are moving to make therapist sexual misconduct with clients a criminal offense. The increased frequency of medical malpractice suits involving sexual misconduct has elevated insurance costs and, in turn, the cost of providing mental health care. Licensing boards and ethics committees are processing ever increasing numbers of claims, and the clinical damage done to the client, as well as the impairment to the mental health professions and to specific practitioners, is staggering. The mental health professions have begun investigating these issues, although with some reluctance if not outright resistance. Research, training, clinical work, and writing by Schoener and his group at the Walk-in Counseling Center in Minneapolis (1989), Pope and Bouhoutsos (1986), Folman (1990), and Lerman (1990) are examples of leadership in confronting the clinical, ethical, legal, educational, and social concerns stemming from therapist sexual misconduct. Resource materials compiled thusfar in this area are significant, including the Minnesota Department of Corrections' handbook for professionals entitled *It's Never OK* (1989); Schoener et al.'s volume entitled *Psychotherapists' Sexual Involvement With Clients* (1989); as well as Lerman's major compilation of resources regarding therapist misconduct (1990). These concerned parties have listened to victims and to impaired providers, have attempted remedies and rehabilitations. The psychotherapy professions are beginning to take responsibility for their own professional violations.

In both public and professional arenas, however, the issues regarding therapist sexual misconduct are often polarized. Therapists, in general, exhibit tendencies to diagnose survivors or to focus on the characteristics of abused clients, such as seductiveness or a childhood sexual abuse history, as major contributors to therapist abuse. Survivors of therapist sexual misconduct, on the other hand, while providing valuable information to the public and to the mental health professions, often at great personal cost, tend to stereotype and distrust therapists and are often discounted by practitioners because of their lack of knowledge about therapeutic processes. Thus, on the one hand, clinical practitioners and social scientists have the ability to participate in discourse in this area, and thus have power, while those people who have experienced the effects of therapist misconduct generally do not have the same ability to contribute to the determination of action.

The purpose of this article is to provide a single-subject account that has one foot in each arena. My ability to participate in this discourse, one that is essential to action, is based on two sets of credentials. The first is that of being a doctoral-level clinical psychologist, licensed in the state of California and in practice for well over a decade. The other is that I am a survivor of not only childhood sexual abuse, but also of therapist sexual misconduct experienced with a doctoral-level clinical psychologist prior to my graduate training. In addition, I had acquired subsequent treatment from other doctoral-level psychologists which proved to be detrimental, both initially and at a later date, and have acquired, fortunately, more recent subsequent treatment which has proven to be corrective. While I am aware of the risks that I take in this public and professional disclosure, I am equally aware of the gains to be made, not only in providing information for the profession, but also hopefully in encouraging other professionals who have had similar experiences–and we do know that there are many–to add their knowledge to this discourse.

To elaborate on my credentials in the professional area, I hold a doctoral degree with dissertation research in the area of attachment and child abuse and have done extensive work in the area of abuse and abuse recovery, including a post-doctoral internship at Children's Hospital in Los Angeles. During my graduate studies I established a professional relationship with Dr. John Bowlby, originator of attachment theory, and was fortunate to receive substantial support from Dr. Bowlby regarding my research and subsequent participation in the area of attachment and child abuse. This included conferences held at Tavistock Centre, authorship of a chapter regarding attachment theory research (DeLozier, 1982), and extensive citation from Dr. Bowlby (for example, *A Secure Base*, 1989). It is significant that throughout this time, while I recognized my own background of separation and loss issues, I had never conceptualized myself as a survivor of abuse. For the last eleven years, I have been a clinical psychologist and Regional Department Head for a major managed healthcare company in Southern California, as well as in private practice. It is notable that my administrative experience has included supervisory responsibilities for a clinician previously accused of sexual misconduct.

Regarding my second set of credentials, my first experience with psychotherapy was at age 29 when my son's school personnel, concerned about his underachievement, referred our family to a psychologist. The therapist's assessment–familiar to us all–was that the kid was fine but that the marriage was in trouble. A few marital sessions, during which the therapist first held my hand as I cried, were followed by a recommendation of individual treatment for my depression. The presenting problems of serious marital, financial, and health stresses were accompanied by my history of parental divorce, childhood sexual abuse, and teenage marriage. Also of importance was my history of critical childhood illness, including rheumatic fever, which left me with the powerful message that I had to follow doctors' orders *literally* to ensure my survival. Thus the unquestioned authority of doctors was paramount. This combination of losses, abuse, and illness had taught me to discredit my own perceptions, needs, and feelings.

While treatment was initially appropriate, the therapist started crossing boundaries of physical contact with behaviors that I now know were clearly not acceptable. For example, an expressed wish for a birthday kiss, with no expectation of such action from him, was met with a statement, "You know I can't do that," followed by a sudden passionate kiss. To say that I was confused is an understatement. Longer and more frequent sessions with progressively more specifically sexual contact, such as fondling my breasts, were followed by the therapist's distancing behavior and attempts at abandonment of treatment. These highly conflictual contacts enormously increased my fears of abandonment and my dependence on the therapist as well as further eroded my attempts to trust my own judgement or emotions.

My initial efforts to obtain outside consultation or subsequent treatment followed my return to college. In increasing distress, I informed one of my psychology professors who referred me for assistance to another university psychology professor. In trepidation, but armed with a newly-discovered magazine containing a cover story about therapist sexual misconduct, I revealed the situation to the second professor, told him I was involved in a therapy which included specific sexual contact and threats of abandonment, and asked for help. With some reference to the State Ethics Committee, this psychologist instructed me not to file a complaint and not to seek legal counsel. He emphasized that the appropriate action would be for the original therapist and myself to be seen in conjoint sessions to work out the problems so "that we could proceed with treatment." This proposed series of sessions in fact took place, with the result that the original treatment was not terminated but was instead implicitly endorsed, became progressively more involved, and continued for years throughout my graduate studies. The facade of treatment continued but included meetings—often late or for many hours—at his office, in my home, and at hotels. The sexual aspects of the relationship included intercourse over a period of years, and an alarm about possible pregnancy for which the therapist scheduled an abortion that fortunately was not needed.

During that period I was separated and then divorced, lost my home, was a single parent of three children, attended graduate school full-time, worked 20 hours a week, and commuted three hours a day. Both therapists attempted marital treatment with my husband and myself. As I became more isolated socially, my support system, already strained by the absence of family nearby and the disruption of married-couple friendships, focused almost exclusively on the therapist. Eventually, believing further attempts at resolution to be futile, I left the therapy relationship and concentrated, as I had in childhood, on what I could control–caring for my family and establishing a career. My one subsequent attempt to broach the problem, with a male colleague, led to the interpretation, "I don't know what you're so upset about. I've had sex with my clients when they needed it." I had reached a place where I could no longer trust clinical intervention in this area.

Gratefully, years later, I was catapulted beyond my entrenched resistance to further treatment by a severe personal relationship crisis. It took, even with my education and training in abuse, *over ten years from my last contact with the initial therapist* to begin to see the extent of the damage resulting from therapist misconduct and to begin recovery. The nature of the damages themselves had prevented my trusting myself or others, and, instead, had heightened my ability to deny the severity of my problems–a technique I had learned as a child. My leap-into-the-dark phone call to another clinician–one of the most difficult things I've ever done–lead finally to subsequent treatment which has proven to be demanding but corrective. In contrast to the isolation, mistrust, secrecy, shame, and guilt engendered by both the initial therapist misconduct and by the further damaging subsequent therapy, my current treatment has addressed the resolution of these problems. This treatment has, however, been expensive, exhausting, at times nearly impossible. It has required an absolute commitment from me that this healing would be done no matter what the cost, even if I lost my home again, had to file bankruptcy, or lost my career. The one exception was that I would not willingly compromise the well being of my children.

Developing trust again in therapy has been difficult and painstaking. Fear of intimacy, anger about previous childhood and adult violations, and disbelief in the trustworthiness of an unknown therapist are but a few of the issues which have prolonged my resistance and testing behavior. I have searched for imperfections in recent therapists, and found some substantial ones. Treatment was severely jeopardized more than once–and my rebuilding with it–by one subsequent therapist's resistance to seeing the extent of the damage, a difficulty resulting from his own violation of appropriate sexual boundaries with at least one other client. My rage at this discovery after two years of treatment, especially when the referral to him had been specifically for treatment of injuries from previous therapist sexual misconduct, was intense. His ensuing denial, rationalization, minimization, blame of and anger toward the client, and abandonment of treatment in a critical situation was severely damaging and, again, the heightened distrust and sense of hopelessness was profound. Highly skilled intervention from specialized experts in psychotherapy, forensics psychology, medicine, and law was essential to my survival of the loss of yet another therapist with my sense of purpose and commitment intact.

Eventually, however, the multiple-approach combination of psychotherapy and consultation with several persistent, committed, and well-trained clinicians; participation in a sexual abuse recovery group and occasionally in a therapist abuse recovery group; healing-through-art and other workshops; appropriate bodywork such as with a certified bioenergetics therapist and with a massage therapist; and taking appropriate action such as filing complaints yielded positive results. I have also had the privilege of direct access to some of the finest resources in this profession, as well as support from expert attorneys, in making decisions and taking action about formal complaint and legal proceedings. Eventually the damage from the previous therapists, as well as from childhood, became evident and began to be repaired. The work has been and continues to be demanding and exhausting beyond what I would have believed, but is also healing and empowering beyond my expectations.

What then have I learned from my experience that is useful to the profession? This personal journey, while adding to my general clinical knowledge about abuse and abuse recovery, also has highlighted issues which call attention to the damage done by unethical therapist behavior, as well as to what is needed for corrective and ethical subsequent treatment. First, it is imperative for clinicians to understand that unethical therapist conduct constitutes an abuse of power. The critical issue in abuse is not so much whether abuse occurs with children or with women or with members of certain ethnic groups, but that the potential for abuse occurs in any relationship in which one party or their role is empowered. In the psychotherapy relationship, as is noted by Brown (1990), "A focus on ethics is a focus on power and how it is used and shared in the process and practices of therapy . . ." (p. 1). Psychotherapists, like parents, are empowered by the nature of their role and are accountable for the responsible handling of the accompanying inherent power differential.

Second, the damage from therapist sexual misconduct in my situation, as in others, is enormous and repeats the dynamics of childhood abuse. Inappropriate subsequent therapy severely compounds the problem. In contrast to one therapist's analogy of searching for a client at the bottom of a well, my perception has been that, after therapist misconduct and damaging subsequent treatment, it is more like searching in an underground labyrinth with hidden passages, secret doors, chains, locks, and bolts. Extensive provisions are needed by both client and clinician for this endeavor.

Third, in my case as in the literature, sexual misconduct by a therapist aborts effective treatment. The guilt and shame from "secret" interaction is generally assumed by the client as boundaries blur and roles are reversed. Isolation, fear of abandonment, excessive concern about therapist approval, and increased dependency lead the client to experience difficulty establishing other relationships, including with another therapist.

Fourth, inappropriate subsequent therapy fails to protect the client who is already suffering from intense distress. Any endorsement–spoken or implied–of sexual touch by the previous clinician increases the client's hopelessness, confusion, and internalization of anger. Maintenance of toxic "secrets" by clinicians, as opposed to privacy and confidentiality, is analogous to the role of the non-protecting parent in an incestuous family. As an example, I had been told by the first subsequent therapist never to tell my husband or anyone else about the relationship between myself and the original therapist. Moreover, furthering the perceived responsibility of the client, such as being told that I would make the best "therapist" that the original therapist could find because I understood him so well, is grossly unethical. If we were to cite comparable physical injuries, we might see on the evening news commentary that a seriously injured accident victim was taken to a hospital, inflicted with additional injuries such as rape or burns by hospital personnel, dismissed from the hospital without treatment, and then billed for the procedure. While this scenario might seem a gross exaggeration to others, in my recovery experience therapist abuse survivors have instantly identified with this description.

What then constitutes responsible subsequent therapy? As a profession we need to address and prevent further clinician abuse but also to assist those who have been previously injured. First, and critically, clients and concerned therapists require permission to talk, to claim their rightful voice. The "no-talk rule" about therapist misconduct must be broken. Clients and the public in general need to be encouraged to bring the problems of our profession and our practitioners to our attention, and we, as therapists, need to respond responsibly. It is only by open dialogue that conflict and mistreatment can be resolved. It is crucial that subsequent therapists convey to the client a sense of concern and non-acceptance of abusive behavior by clinicians. Failure to do so extends the cycle of abuse.

Subsequent therapy also needs to grant the client permission to grieve the multiple losses and injuries previously sustained. The betrayal by and loss of a previous therapist, in addition to the original reasons for treatment, requires grief work. This is the loss of yet another attachment figure. Resolution includes the processing of many, many layers of anger and sadness. Therapists treating previously abused clients can expect delays in the development of trust and often clients cannot trust a therapist of the same gender as the abuser. The client's protective stance is appropriate and necessary given previous experience. Any development of intimacy in the therapeutic relationship will elicit fears of repeated abuse or abandonment because the nurturing sought by the client has previously been accompanied by abuse. The resulting approach/avoidance conflict is severe, as it is in the case of abused children who nevertheless need their parents' caretaking.

When clients become able to express anger about previous violations, there will be rage and more rage. The client will doubt the therapist's capacity to manage the intense anger. It is imperative that treating clinicians be able and willing to, first, own responsibility for their own shortcomings and work to correct them and, second, acknowledge the clients' right to feel enraged and to express rage in appropriate ways. Knowledge about abuse recovery and crisis management is essential.

In my experience, since abuse is largely nonverbal, recovery includes nonverbal as well as verbal aspects of healing. The behavioral communications between clinician and client are therefore critical in psychotherapy with previously abused clients. This raises the very important issue of the use of touch in therapy. While I consider the use of *appropriate touch at the discretion of the client* to be a powerful aspect of healing, it is crucial that the clinician fully understand that any touch occurs within the context of and heightens the transferential relationship. Furthermore, the handling of the therapeutic relationship–in both its transferential and counter-transferential aspects–is the sole responsibility of the therapist. "Touching revives all the repressed feelings in the body and is not a panacea. It revives hope but it also revives pain, rage, and despair" (Hilton, 1990). This is true for the clinician as well as for the client. ". . . Prohibition does not stop acting out, even when your reputation and career are at stake . . . The greatest safeguard against the misuse of touch is to know your own responses and boundaries in regard to touching and being touched" (Hilton, 1990). Therefore, it is essential that any practitioner who uses touch in any psychotherapy, and certainly with abuse survivors, be specifically and adequately trained in this area.

Clearly, emphatically, any touch must be *only* at the choice of the client, affirmative with clear and firm boundaries both in its intent and in its effect, not sexual in nature, and not shame-producing. It is always the responsibility of the clinician to maintain appropriate boundaries. Unless the practitioner is trained in and has a solid understanding of the powerful dynamics of touch in psychotherapy, has a thorough knowledge of her or his own responses to touch, and is certain of her or his ability to adhere to clearly-acceptable boundaries, the practitioner should not utilize touch in psychotherapy. Nurturing touch can be obtained by clients in other modalities, if and when the client is ready. Group work with other survivors of abuse, dance and movement therapy, massage therapy–all by impeccably ethical practitioners–could provide possibilities for contact as well as other support if the client is amenable to these adjuncts to therapy.

Since the client has difficulty trusting herself or himself, the therapist's support of the client's decisions regarding actions such as complaints or legal procedures is crucial. Just as an example, confronting the serious restrictions of the statutes of limitations–given the incapacitating nature of the damages–is a source of major frustration. The client feels as if they had been like a medical patient expected to report malpractice while in a surgeon-induced coma. The responsibility of the treating clinician is to assist the client, not to create further enmeshment, not to overprotect, and certainly not to harm or hold the client back because of the clinician's own problems or fears about ethical or legal issues. Empowerment of the client is the treatment objective. As a client, I have learned first-hand how incredibly difficult the process of taking action is and why so few survivors do so. The time, energy, and other resources needed in the grievance process taxes even the strongest survivor. However, growth comes, where possible, from directing pain and anger into appropriate action. Support needs to be extended also to the secondary victims–family and loved ones who have been and continue to be greatly affected.

Therapists treating survivors of previous therapist abuse undertake a demanding assignment. It is my strong recommendation that treatment not be managed in isolation. The client needs a support network from multiple sources. So does the clinician. A multiple-therapist or team approach is helpful; referral of the client for adjunctive services such as medical, legal, advocacy, or community services is essential. Likewise, the treating clinician needs access to and encouragement to utilize support services such as legal or clinical consultation, supervision, and continuing education in this area.

As a profession concerned with proactive change, it is crucial for our practitioners to be trained and supported in addressing common ethical issues, avoiding misconduct, and in remedying problems resulting from prior abuse. It is not sufficient for ethical standards to set least-common-denominator requirements or for clinical training programs to ignore or minimize the likely pitfalls which lead to therapist misconduct. Licensure-required training in ethics and professional issues, including attention to responsible therapist boundaries and to issues related to sexual misconduct, and the development of a professional network including professionals who have experienced the effects of therapist misconduct, seem essential steps toward prevention and recovery.

In conclusion, while we can recognize the difficulty in seeing and addressing the ethical problems of our profession, the courage to do so follows a time-honored path to healing. Angeles Arrien (1991), a cross-cultural anthropologist, teaches about what she regards as "universal wisdom," meaning knowledge held and taught in at least 85% of known indigenous cultures. She emphasizes that traditionally wisdom is to be gleaned from woundedness, that woundedness hides resources, and that facing and mastering our own shadows–our fears and doubts–allows each unique individual to contribute her or his "original medicine" to the world. According to native wisdom, an ordinary healer can use positive influence to help others, but the truly powerful healer–the shaman–has, in facing and mastering internal negative influences, learned also to confront and transform them in others. *This is our work.*

In addressing the issues of abuse and misconduct within our profession, we follow the pathway of the peaceful warrior whose competition is within her- or himself and whose path to knowledge is through the courage to face her or his own limitations. In the words of a Native American Indian prayer:

Grandfather,
I do ask for death,
For the parts of me,   *Grandmother,*
That will not hear   *Give me birth again,*
Or speak the truth,   *With love as my guide,*
Which are too blind to see. *Truth and Beauty as my path,*
                              With nothing left to hide. (Sams, 1990)

And therein is my message and my hope, calling this profession and its practitioners to the challenge of addressing our own woundedness, the injuries we both sustain and perpetuate. It is the challenge to follow the time-honored indigenous wisdom and to thereby claim and contribute our even-greater powers to understand and to be healers of ourselves, our clients, and our profession.

REFERENCES

Arrien, A. (1993). *The four fold way.* New York: Harpers/Collins Publishers.

Bowlby, J. (1988). *A secure base.* New York: Basic Books.

Brown, L. (ed.) "A Feminist Framework for Ethical Theory." In: Lerman, H. and Porter, N. (eds.) (1990). Feminist ethics in psychotherapy. New York: Springer Publication Co., pp. 1-3.

DeLozier, P.P. (1982). "Attachment theory and child abuse." In Parkes, C.M. & Stevenson-Hinde, J. (Eds) (pp. 95-117). *The place of attachment in human behavior.* New York: Basic Books.

Folman, R. (1990). Legislative action on therapist misconduct: Implications for treatment. Paper presented at the American Psychological Association Convention, New Orleans.

Heilbrun, C.G. (1988). Writing a woman's life. New York: Ballantine Books.

Hilton, R. (1990). *Touching in psychotherapy.* Edmonds, Washington: Pacific Northwest Bioenergetics Conference.

Lerman, H. (1990). *Sexual intimacies between psychotherapists and patients: An annotated bibliography of mental health, legal, and public media literature and relevant legal cases* (2nd Ed.). Phoenix, Arizona: Division of Psychotherapy of the American Psychological Association.

Pope, K.S., & Bouhoutsos, J.C. (1986). *Sexual intimacy between therapists and patients.* New York: Praeger Publishers.

Sanderson, B.E. (Ed.) (1989). *It's never OK: A handbook for professionals on sexual exploitation by counselors and therapists.* St. Paul, Minnesota: Minnesota Department of Corrections.

Schoener, G.R., Milgrom, J.H., Gonsiorek, J.C., Luepker, E.T., & Conroe, R.M. (1989). *Psychotherapists' sexual involvement with clients.* Minneapolis, Minnesota: Walk-In Counseling Center.

Comparing the Experiences
of Women Clients
Sexually Exploited by Female
versus Male Psychotherapists

Mindy Benowitz

In reviewing the research on sexual exploitation of clients by therapists one finds that it is focused almost exclusively on male psychotherapists' abuse of female clients. Female therapist-female client sexual exploition has only been addressed in a limited number of anecdotal reports (Applebaum, 1987; Brown, 1985, 1987, 1988, 1989; Gartrell and Sanderson, 1992; Gonsiorek, 1989; Rigby, 1986; Sonne, Meyer, Borys, & Marshall, 1985). There has been no systematic, empirical research on the impact and dynamics of women psychotherapists' sexual abuse of their female clients. The reported prevalence of female therapist-female client sexual contact varies

Mindy Benowitz, PhD, is a licensed psychologist in private practice in Minneapolis, MN. She is past Vice Chair of Minnesota Women Psychologists. She has written about heterosexism and lesbian battering and has lectured on sexual exploitation by therapists, boundary issues in psychotherapy, eating disorders, and sexual abuse. This article is based on Dr. Benowitz's 1991 PhD dissertation entitled "Sexual Exploitation of Female Clients by Female Psychotherapists: Interviews with Clients and a Comparison to Women Exploited by Male Psychotherapists."

Correspondence may be addressed to Dr. Benowitz at 1730 Clifton Place, Suite 205, Minneapolis, MN 55403.

[Haworth co-indexing entry note]: "Comparing the Experiences of Women Clients Sexually Exploited by Female versus Male Psychotherapists." Benowitz, Mindy. Co-published simultaneously in Women & Therapy (The Haworth Press, Inc.) Vol. 15, No. 1, 1994, pp. 69-83; and Bringing Ethics Alive: Feminist Ethics in Psychotherapy Practice (ed: Nanette K. Gartrell) The Haworth Press, Inc., 1994, pp. 69-83. Multiple copies of this article/chapter may be purchased from The Haworth Document Delivery Center [1-800-3-HAWORTH; 9:00 a.m. - 5:00 p.m. (EST)].

from 1% to 12% of female therapists. Averaging survey results on female therapists' self-report of sexual contact with female clients (Holroyd and Brodsky, 1977; Gartrell, Herman, Olarte, Feldstein, & Localio, 1986; Lyn, 1990) yields 4%. When one averages the studies that include female clients' reports of sexual contact with their female therapists (Schoener, Milgrom, & Gonsiorek, 1984; Friedeman, 1981; Russell, 1984), the percentage is increased to 7%.

Research is needed to explore common characteristics shared by clients who are sexually exploited by female therapists, determine whether the process of exploitation and its impact differ according to the therapist's gender, and assess which variables affect the emotional impact of the exploitation. A systematic comparison of female and male exploitative therapists, as well as clients and therapists of different sexual orientations, could also shed light on the impact or process of the exploitation. This article reports on a study of these issues (Benowitz, 1991).

The purpose of the current study was to examine the experiences of women who had verbal or physical sexual contact with a female psychotherapist or counselor. Major topics examined included characteristics of the participants and of the therapists, characteristics of the sexualized therapy relationships, the impact on the participants, and comparisons with women who had sexual contact with male therapists.[1]

Fifteen women were interviewed. During the interview the participants also completed three Symptoms Check Lists (SCLs) pertaining to the few weeks after the relationship ended, a baseline time prior to the relationship, and the time of the interview. The interviews and the SCLs were based in part on Vinson's (1984) research, which allows comparisons with her data on women exploited by male psychotherapists.[2] The results and their implications are discussed in each section.

CLIENT CHARACTERISTICS

This study explored potential commonalities of the participants, such as history of physical and sexual abuse, sexual orientation, and general demographic factors. The participants were Caucasian and averaged 36 years of age. Thirteen of the 15 women had at least 16 years of formal education; 7 had graduate degrees. Interestingly, one third ($n = 5$) were in training to be or were practicing mental health professionals at the time of the exploitative therapy. The high level of education and the number of mental health professionals among the participants supports the notion that simply being in the client role is inherently vulnerable. Although there was a wide range in the participants' level of daily functioning, the data clearly show that education and competence do not necessarily protect clients from harm by therapists. The data support current ethical and legal guidelines that client consent is not an adequate defense for sexual contact with clients.

One might speculate that survivors of childhood abuse are more vulnerable to later exploitation by a therapist. In this sample, 80% of the participants ($n = 12$) reported childhood sexual abuse and 80% reported childhood physical abuse. However, since a history of childhood abuse is quite high among clients in general, and there are exploited clients who have not been previously abused, it is premature to conclude that childhood victimization predisposes clients to further sexual exploitation.

One factor that may have increased the participants' vulnerability to exploitation by a female therapist was the participants' need to discuss sexual orientation issues. Many of them were in the process of questioning and re-identifying their sexual orientation. For seven–almost half–this was their first sexual relationship with a woman. It appears that the stage of exploring a bisexual or lesbian identity and openly discussing it in therapy may be risky for clients whose therapists are prone to abuse.

THERAPIST CHARACTERISTICS

Therapists from all backgrounds and types of training have been reported to be sexual with clients. Research (Borys and Pope, 1989) has shown relatively proportional rates of sexual contact with clients among social workers, psychiatrists, and psychologists. The female therapists in this study included psychologists ($n = 6$), social workers ($n = 2$), pastoral counselors ($n = 3$), marriage and family therapists ($n = 1$), and those with non-traditional or of unknown training ($n = 3$). Two worked in sexual assault programs.

Most of the therapists ($n = 10$) in this study were older than the participants, by an average of 11 years. This is similar to male therapists who sexually exploit clients (Butler, 1975; Dahlberg, 1970; Callan, 1987), although it holds true for therapy in general (Friedeman, 1981). The therapists averaged five years in practice at the time of the sexualized therapy. Two had Ph.D. degrees, ten had masters degrees, and three had B.A.'s.

The data clearly dispute the notion that sexual contact between female therapists and female clients is a one-time, harmless case of two women who just happened to fall in love. Over half ($n = 8$; 53%) of the participants had heard that the therapist had also been overtly sexually involved with another client at some point. This number reflects only those cases the participants knew of (often from therapist disclosure) and therefore probably underestimates the actual number of repeat offenders among these therapists. The percentage of repeat offenders reported in this study is lower than some reports of primarily male therapists and female clients (Holroyd & Brodsky, 1977: 80%; Butler, 1975: 70%) and higher than other reports (Gartrell et al., 1986: 33%).

Regarding sexual orientation, one fifth of the therapists were reportedly heterosexual, one fifth bisexual, two fifths lesbian, and one fifth reportedly said nothing to the participants about their sexual orientation. One third of the therapists were married to men during the participants' therapy. Both the covert and overt categories of sexual relationships included therapists who identified as heterosexual, bisexual, and lesbian. The diversity of sexual orientations among the therapists validates anecdotal reports (Brown, 1988; Rigby & Sophie, 1990; Gonsiorek, 1989) that a heterosexual orientation or being in a committed relationship with a man are not clear predictors that female therapists will refrain from sexual contact with female clients.

The data also support the anecdotal literature (Brown, 1985; Gartrell & Sanderson, 1992) indicating that therapists who are not comfortable with their feelings of same-sex attraction may be at higher risk for acting inappropriately with their clients. Over one third of the therapists were described as demonstrating conflict about their sexual behavior with women and 20% of the therapists ($n = 3$) told the participant that this was their first same-sex involvement.

The descriptions of the therapists' shame due to heterosexism are based on the clients' observations and memories of therapists' comments, and might be higher if one were able to study the therapists directly. One sharp example of internalized oppression was one of the pastoral counselors, who demonstrated enormous conflict about being sexual with a woman. The participant reported that the last time they had sexual contact, the counselor "said she was praying for God to kill us" (Benowitz, 1991, p. 75). This participant also cited examples to support her belief that the counselor encouraged her to kill herself. Discomfort with same-sex attractions was not a universal theme, however. Several of the therapists were open about being lesbian and did not appear to the participants to feel uncomfortable with their sexual orientation.

To prevent sexual abuse of female clients, all female therapists must become comfortable with whatever same-sex attractions they feel. This could decrease therapists' sexual experimentation with clients, with whom sex may seem safer and more hidden than with peers. It would also increase the likelihood of using supervision more effectively for cases in which one is vulnerable to acting on sexual feelings toward clients.

The literature on sexual exploitation by male therapists indicates that experiencing high stress in their personal lives, such as ending a relationship may increase therapists' vulnerability to sexual acting out with clients (Butler & Zelen, 1977). Slightly over half of the therapists ($n = 8$) in this study reportedly experienced a major change in their relationship status (mostly break-ups) during the sexualized therapy. Some of the therapists may have sought reassurance of their attractiveness and self-worth from their clients.

CHARACTERISTICS OF THE EXPLOITATIVE RELATIONSHIPS

Sexual exploitation exists on a continuum that begins with poor judgment, proceeds to covert exploitation, and ends with overt sexual exploitation. The eleven overtly sexual dyads in this study all included breast and/or genital contact. Covert sexual contact in this study consisted of flirting, sexualized talk and physical contact without touching of obviously sexual parts of either body. Four of the therapists were categorized as covertly sexually exploitative and had behaviors such as flirting and types of touch commonly shared by lovers (e.g., kissing; very long, full hugs). One of the covertly exploited participants described how over the course of their therapy, the counselor joked about the two of them running away to get married, had lain on the floor at the end of a session and made "flirtatious" or "coy" comments to the participant, held the participant's hand during sessions and played with her jewelry, stroked her hair, mentioned watching pornographic movies the previous night and feeling aroused by them, and stood and talked while hugging at the end of sessions with her face very close to the participant's. Due to the absence of overtly sexual touch, the participant doubted her own perceptions. When she attempted to discuss the sexual dynamics, the therapist reportedly denied her own role and would only focus on the participant's sexual attraction to the therapist. A second woman described frequently receiving full, long hugs from the therapist, sometimes with accompanying back rubs. After the participant asked to be held by the therapist, the therapist was described as having pulled the client to her while on the couch and "crushed (the client) into her" (Benowitz, 1991, p. 82). This therapist would also tell the participant details of her sex life, such as describing a female friend's genitals and telling the client about advice she received to improve her own sex life.

The dynamics of the overt and covert relationships were similar in most respects. The participants in each group described the same types and same intensities of feelings. Both groups commonly expressed feeling in love with the therapist, feeling that this was a very important relationship to them, and feeling betrayed and used later on. However, those who experienced covert and no overt sexual contact from their therapists had much more difficulty identifying the exploitation. The occurrence of nonsexual boundary violations helped them take their discomfort about the sexual dynamics more seriously.

There were several themes in the exploitative relationships. The relationships tended to be of a secretive, affair nature. In 8 of the 11 overtly sexual dyads, the therapist and/or the client were also involved with someone else. Socializing with the client was common for the overtly sexual therapists. Seven of these 11 dyads kept the sexual nature of the relationship hidden, pretending to just be friends. Three of the overtly sexual therapists were violent with the clients–two were sexually violent and one was physically abusive. The covertly sexual therapists in this study did not socialize with the participants outside of sessions.

Physical touch was common in the therapy itself, but not universal. The therapists tended to initiate the touch and did so under the pretext of comforting the clients. This tended to progress to more intense, covertly sexual touch and then to overt sexual contact. Although all but one of the relationships were described as important love relationships, only one fit the pattern described by Rigby (1986) of committed, primary relationships in which the couple intended to or did live together.

Sexual exploitation involves a series of decisions and behaviors that show a pattern of poor boundaries on the therapist's part. In order to identify precursors to sexual exploitation, the participants were asked if, in retrospect, they could identify hints that the therapy would become sexual. Almost all of the participants ($n = 13$) could identify hints.

Common hints involved the therapist's body language ($n = 13, 87\%$). Examples of these included touching the client's legs or hands, the therapist sitting in a way that revealed sexual parts of her body, affectionate touching that felt sexual to the client, much holding of the client in sessions, hugs that felt like "a lover hug and not a friend hug." The second most frequent precursors were comments made by the therapists ($n = 9, 60\%$). Being told that she was a favorite or "special" client was often cited as a retrospective hint.

Another hint involved the blurring of therapeutic boundaries such as the choice of setting for therapy and socializing with the client ($n = 8, 53\%$). Examples included the therapist asking the participant out to dinner, talking about therapy issues in informal settings, using the therapist's bedroom as an office with the client seated on the bed, and disclosing their own problems to the client. When asked specifically about self-disclosure, 14 of the 15 participants said that the therapists discussed their personal problems in ways that seemed very inappropriate. This began prior to the sexual contact in all but 2 cases.

Exploitative therapists also exhibited seductive behavior ($n = 6$;

40%), such as flirting or offering the client a hug and then giving her a five-minute backrub along with the hug.

In comparing the precursor data to Vinson's data on male therapist-female client sexual exploitation, similar percentages of participants could retrospectively identify hints that the therapy would become sexual and similar types of hints were cited.

In an attempt to learn how exploitative therapists justify their sexual behavior with clients, the participants were asked if the therapist ever commented about mixing sex and therapy. Nearly half ($n = 7$, 47%) never commented on the matter. Of those who did comment, the most common justification was that the sexual contact would help the participants, reported by eight (53%) women. Explicit messages that the therapist was reparenting the participant were recounted by four (27%) women, and another five (33%) said that similar messages were given with a less specific framework. One participant's statement is typical of several responses: "she said that all my past relationships have been so harmful, and she wanted to teach me how to have a healthy relationship, how to get close to people" (Benowitz, 1991, p. 91). Other ways the therapists said they were helping the clients were by modeling talking openly about sexual matters and by being a guide in the coming out process.

Four therapists (27%) said it was permissible to be sexual with the client because they were not in a counselor role, either due to terminating therapy or to having a grassroots orientation such as working in a sexual assault program. In the four cases in which the therapist cited the termination justification, the participants described a clear sexual dynamic during therapy, and three of the four discussed sexual attraction and desires for a relationship while conducting the therapy. A final type of comment about mixing sex and therapy involved admitting that it was wrong to be sexual with the client but doing it anyway.

The results on precursors and types of justifications imply a need to educate therapists about the ongoing nature of transference and about responsibilities therapists continue to hold after termination. They also imply a need for all types of counselors to acknowledge being in a counselor role with people they help in any organized, systematic way. The therapists' justifications show a great deal of denial about power dynamics and their own sexual dynamics in therapy and point to the need for all therapists to learn more about their own sexual dynamics which could lead to sexualizing clients. The data also underscore the need to educate mental health professionals about the harm caused by sexualizing the therapy relationship.

Comparing the male and female psychotherapists on the dynamics and process of sexual exploitation yields several interesting observations. The female therapists' justifications are quite similar to the beliefs of sexually exploitative male therapists, who have a tendency to believe that sexual contact is less harmful and more beneficial to the client than do therapists who do not have sexual contact with clients (Gartrell et al., 1986; Derosis, Hamilton, Morrison, & Strauss 1987; Twemblow & Gabbard, 1989). However, the majority of (mostly male) offenders in these studies knew it was harmful to the clients and did it anyway.

The common scenario in sexual exploitation of female clients is that the therapist initiates the sexual contact. This was even more pronounced among the female therapists in the present study than among the male therapists in Vinson's study. Ninety-three percent of the female therapists were described as having initiated the sexual contact, compared to 72% of the male therapists. Furthermore, the female therapists began the sexual contact earlier in the therapy relationship than did the male therapists in Vinson's study (averages of 6.5 months versus 9 months). This contradicts the stereotype of more mutual participation and equal power in female therapist-female client sexual contact.

Heterosexism and the belief that women in general are not abusive led many women to discount their perceptions of sexual dynamics. For example, one woman stated, "I was curious about whether this was OK or not. If this were a man, I would have gotten it after the second session. It didn't fit my belief system regarding women. So (I'd like) more information that women can also be perpetrators, can be inappropriate too" (Benowitz, 1991, p. 112).

Many participants in the current study described fear that others would not believe them, and also received comments that discounted the impact and the exploitative nature of the relationship. Fear of other's heterosexist judgments also increased the clients' isolation and impeded them from seeking redress. A participant stated, "I wish, if I could change anything [about resources available to help them cope], it would be that people would accept lesbianism as OK, because that's what compounded what went on. It was why I had to keep so much secret. It was one more added thing to deal with" (Benowitz, 1991, p. 112). Heterosexism may have led some therapists to confuse nurturing feelings with sexual feelings, or to mislabel their own behaviors with clients.

The results illustrate the importance of eliminating heterosexism on individual and societal levels. Eradicating heterosexism would decrease exploited clients' shame and isolation, allowing them to recognize the exploitation sooner, be more likely to get help, and seek redress more often. This in turn would increase accountability and consequences for exploitative therapists.

A final difference in the dynamics of the exploitative relationships was that the female dyads tended to socialize more openly than the male-female dyads. In Vinson's study, the male-female dyads never blended their social lives. However, in the present study 10 of the 11 dyads who socialized together did so with the therapist's friends or family, although they often hid the sexual nature of the relationship. It may be that the heterosexist assumption that sex occurs only between males and females allowed the female dyads to "get away with" being social in public. When men and women socialize together, a sexual relationship is more often suspected. It is also possible that community norms permitted social relationships between female therapists and female clients.

IMPACT ON CLIENTS

Nearly all of the women in this study described varying degrees of harmful impact from the sexual contact and concomitant boundary violations. The most painful period occurred immediately after the relationship ended. Post-traumatic Stress Disorder (PTSD) (American Psychiatric Association, 1987) was very common after the therapy or relationship ended, experienced by three fourths of the participants ($n = 11$). Fourteen of the 15 women (93%) said that the relationship worsened the problems for which they originally sought help, by intensifying the issues, by postponing attending to them, and/or by creating new issues in addition to the original ones.

The negative impact was quite long-lasting for many participants. The average length of time elapsed since the sexualized therapy was seven years. As a group, the participants had fewer symptoms at the time of the interview than they described having at the end of the exploitative relationship. However, two thirds of the women said they were worse off—endorsed more symptoms on the SCL—an average of seven years after the sexualized therapy than at a baseline time before the therapy began. Four women (27%) still had PTSD.

The women also described various ways that the relationship continued to impact on their lives. Over half described experiencing intense anger and betrayal feelings ($n = 10$; 67%), decreased trust in people in general ($n = 11$; 73%), and depression and feelings of abandonment ($n = 9$; 60%). Two thirds said the relationship hurt their view of themselves as sexual partners and increased their feelings of inadequacy and their fears of being vulnerable. Forty percent ($n = 6$) reported still struggling with guilt and shame about positive feelings about the relationship and/or self-blame for the relationship.

The relationship's impact on the participants' feelings about their sexual orientation were quite varied and almost evenly divided among four themes: (1) the relationship had little or no effect on the women's feelings about their sexual orientation; (2) the relationship helped them to acknowledge or validate a lesbian or bisexual identity (two of these four women felt regret and conflict that this occurred with their therapist as opposed to someone else); (3) the relationship led participants to feel less trusting of women in general, and therefore made them less comfortable with their lesbian or bisexual identity; (4) the relationship increased their feelings of confusion regarding their previously held sexual orientation, both heterosexual and lesbian.

The sexualized relationship also increased the clients' mistrust and cynicism about therapy and therapists for 12 (80%) of the participants. Almost half of the group indicated that subsequent therapy helped them to regain their trust of some therapists. For those who sought further psychotherapy, the sexualized therapy appeared to influence the participants' choice of the gender and/or sexual orientation of subsequent therapists, although who they felt safe with varied greatly among the participants. It is interesting that some participants believed that seeking a heterosexually-identified female therapist would provide them with automatic protection from future sexual exploitation. The results of this study challenge this assumption.

Positive effects coexisted with negative effects for nine participants, including feeling more attractive (20%) and learning more about boundary/power issues which subsequently helped them in their personal and work lives (33%). Positive feelings toward the therapist and/or the sexual contact contributed to later guilt feelings for many participants.

This study provides some preliminary data on factors which may affect the impact on the client of sexual exploitation by a female therapist. Due to the small sample size, the results of these analyses must be viewed as trends which need further validation, but provide interesting information for present consideration and future research.

First, the vast majority of participants experienced similarly high levels of symptoms after the relationships ended, and varied more in the types and degrees of symptoms at the time of the interview. This indicates that specific variables may have a greater effect on the long-term rather than the short-term impact of the relationships.

Second, the results suggest that covert sexual relationships have the same degree of harm as overt sexual relationships. There were no significant differences statistically or qualitatively between participants whose therapists were covertly versus overtly sexual on any of the impact variables tested (the number of symptoms when the relationship ended, current feelings about therapists and therapy in general, impact on the participants' original problems, and whether they ever considered filing a complaint). Covert sexual exploitation is probably much more common than overt, and deserves more attention in future research.

Third, the results suggest that shorter, less intense therapeutic relationships without ongoing and pervasive sexual dynamics during the course of therapy may contribute to a less negative impact. For example, analyses indicated trends such that more therapy sessions before the sexual contact began were related to more symptoms when the relationship ended (r (14) = .425, p = .11) and at the time of the interview (r (14) = .40, p = .14). Also, the longer therapy continued after the sexual contact began, the more symptoms participants reported experiencing after the relationship ended (r (15) = .59, p = .11) and at the time of the interview (r (15) = .64, p < .05). This suggests that continuing the therapy after the initiation of sexual contact increases the negative impact of the experience. Terminating the therapy did not prevent negative consequences, however.

The impact of the exploitative relationships on the participants in this study was remarkably similar to the women in Vinson's (1984) study who were sexually exploited by male therapists. The percentages were nearly identical for the two groups of participants on the following variables: the number of participants experiencing each SCL symptom; the incidence of PTSD in the few weeks after the relationship ended (this study: 67%; Vinson: 64%); the negative impact on the participants' feelings about therapists and therapy in general (this study: 80%; Vinson: 86%); the negative impact on their original problems (this study: 68%; Vinson: 87%); and their "very negative" evaluation rating of the relationship (this study: 60%; Vinson: 59%); impaired personal relationships, difficulty trusting people, and discomfort with sex (this study: 60%; Vinson: 59%); and feelings of guilt and shame (each study: 40%). Furthermore, Vinson's data also indicated that for women exploited by male therapists, a brief sexual involvement was necessary but not sufficient to avoid PTSD after the relationship ended.

CONCLUSION

The results of this study show that sexual exploitation of female clients usually produces lasting harm to clients. Female therapists from all counseling disciplines and sexual orientations sexually exploit their female clients. Recognizing the existence and impact of the problem is an important first step in preventing future abuse.

NOTES

1. The study also examined participants' use of redress procedures, which are not summarized in this article.

2. Vinson's 22 female participants included one woman whose exploitative therapist was female. Data from this participant was deleted from analyses when possible.

REFERENCES

American Psychiatric Association. (1987). *Diagnostic and Statistical Manual of Mental Illness III, Revised.*

Applebaum, Gail (1987, January). Consequences of sexual exploition of clients. Paper presented at Boundary Dilemmas in the Client-Therapist Relationship: A Working Conference for Lesbian Therapists, Los Angeles, CA.

Benowitz, M. (1991). Sexual Exploitation of female clients by female psychotherapists: Interviews with clients and a comparison to women exploited by male psychotherapists. University Microfilms Inc., Ann Arbor, MI.

Borys, D., & Pope, K. (1989). Dual relationships between therapists and clients: A national study of psychologists, psychiatrists, and social workers. *Professional Psychology: Research and Practice, 20* (5), 283-293.

Brown, L. S. (1985). Power, responsibility, boundaries: Ethical concerns for the lesbian feminist therapist. *Lesbian Ethics,* 1(3), 30-45.

Brown, L. S. (1987a, January). Learning to think about ethics: A guide for the perplexed lesbian feminist therapist. Keynote speech presented at the Los Angeles Chapter of the Association for Women in Psychology Conference, Boundary Dilemmas for the Lesbian Feminist Therapist, Los Angeles, CA.

Brown, L. S. (1987b, August). Beyond thou shalt not: Developing conceptual frameworks for ethical decision-making. Paper presented at a symposium of the 95th Convention of the American Psychological Association, Ethical and Boundary Issues For Lesbians and Gay Psychotherapists, New York City, NY.

Brown, L. S. (1988). Harmful effects of post-termination sexual and romantic relationships between therapists and their former clients. *Psychotherapy,* 25(2), 249-255.

Brown, L. S. (1989, Fall). Ask Dr. Practice: A column for feminist practitioners. *Psychology of Women: Newsletter of Division 35, American Psychological Association,* 15(4).

Butler, S.E. (1975). Sexual contact between therapists and patients. University Microfilms International, Ann Arbor, MI (No. 76-10, 411).

Butler, S. E., & Zelen, S. L. (1977). Sexual intimacies between therapists and patients. *Psychotherapy: Theory, Research, and Practice,* 14(2), 139-145.

Callan, S. R. (1987). *Sexual exploitation in the treatment setting: A study of female survivors.* Unpublished master's thesis. Smith College School of Social Work, North Hampton, MA.

Dahlberg, C. C. (1970). Sexual contact between patient and therapist. *Contemporary Psychoanalysis,* 6(2), 107-124.

Derosis, H., Hamilton, J. A., Morrison, E., & Strauss, M. (1987). More on psychiatrist-patient sexual contact. *American Journal of Psychiatry,* 144(5), 688-689.

Friedeman, S. D. (1981). *The effects of sexual contact between therapist and client on psychotherapy outcome.* University Microfilms International, Ann Arbor, MI (No. 8309699).

Gartrell, N., & Sanderson, B. (1992). Sexual abuse of women by women in psychotherapy: Counseling and advocacy. *Women & Therapy (special issue).*

Gartrell, N., Herman, J., Olarte, S., Feldstein, M., & Localio, R. (1986). Psychiatrist-patient sexual contact: Results of a national survey, I: Prevalence. *American Journal of Psychiatry*, 143(9), 1126-1131.

Gonsiorek, J. C. (1989). Sexual exploitation by psychotherapists: Some observations on male victims and on sexual orientation concerns. In B. E. Sanderson (Ed.), *It's never OK: A handbook for professionals on sexual exploitation by counselors and therapists* (pp. 95-99). St. Paul, MN: Minnesota Department of Corrections.

Holroyd, J. & Brodsky, A. (1977). Psychologists' attitudes toward and practices regarding erotic and non-erotic physical contact with patients. *American Psychologist*, 32(10), 843-849.

Lyn, L. (1990). *Life in the fishbowl: Lesbian and gay therapists social interactions with their clients.* Unpublished master's thesis, Southern Illinois University, Carbondale.

Rigby, D. (1986, March). *Sexual involvement of women therapists with their women clients.* Paper presented at the 11th National Conference of the Association of Women in Psychology, Oakland, CA.

Rigby, D. N., & Sophie, J. (1990). Ethical issues and client sexual preference. In H. Lerman, & N. Porter (Eds.) *Feminist ethics in psychotherapy* (pp. 165-175). New York: Springer.

Russell, R. (1984). *Social workers' awareness of and response to the problem of sexual contact between clients and helping professionals.* Unpublished master's thesis, University of Washington, Seattle.

Schoener, G. R., Milgrom, J. H., & Gonsiorek, J. (1984). Sexual exploitation of clients by therapists. *Women & Therapy*, 3(3/4), 63-69.

Sonne, J., Meyer, C. B., Borys, D., & Marshall, V. (1985). Clients' reactions to sexual intimacy in therapy. *American Journal of Orthopsychiatry*, 55, 183-189.

Twemblow, S.W. & Gabbard, G.O. (1989). The lovesick therapist. In G.O. Gabbard (ed.), *Sexual exploitation in professional relationships* (pp. 71-87). Washington, D.C.: American Psychiatric Press.

Vinson, J. S. (1984). *Sexual contact with psychotherapists: A study of client reactions and complaint procedures.* Unpublished doctoral dissertation, California School of Professional Psychology, Berkeley.

The Practice of Ethics Within Feminist Therapy

Hannah Lerman

ETHICAL CONCERN WITHIN FEMINIST THERAPY

The Feminist Therapy Institute (FTI) does not encompass all of feminist therapy, but it has had a significant impact upon the field (Rosewater & Walker, 1985; Lerman & Porter, 1990a; Brown and Root, 1990). How FTI has dealt with feminist ethical issues is therefore instructive. The Feminist Therapy Institute has been greatly concerned with ethics as an organization because a large number of its members have been concerned about ethics. One can see that in the nature of the presentations each year at the Advanced Feminist Therapy Institutes and in the process by which the FTI ethics code was formulated (Rave & Larsen, 1990). The emphasis can be seen in the nature of the ethical issues discussed in the papers from its very first year (Bravo & Walker, 1985). One could say that our comprehensive view of ethics has something to do with fully extending the statement "the personal is political" into feminist therapy practice.

Hannah Lerman has written about feminist therapy for many years. She has had a long-term interest in ethics and is a clinical psychologist in practice in Los Angeles. She is the author of *A Mote in Freud's Eye: From Psychoanalysis to the Psychology of Women* and an editor of *Feminist Ethics in Psychotherapy.*

Correspondence may be addressed to Dr. Lerman at 10509 Rose Avenue, Los Angeles, CA 90034.

[Haworth co-indexing entry note]: "The Practice of Ethics Within Feminist Therapy." Lerman, Hannah. Co-published simultaneously in *Women & Therapy* (The Haworth Press, Inc.) Vol. 15, No. 1, 1994, pp. 85-92; and *Bringing Ethics Alive: Feminist Ethics in Psychotherapy* (ed: Nanette K. Gartrell) The Haworth Press, Inc., 1994, pp. 85-92. Multiple copies of this article/chapter may be purchased from The Haworth Document Delivery Center [1-800-3-HAWORTH; 9:00 a.m. - 5:00 p.m. (EST)].

Even before the Feminist Therapy Institute was formed in 1982, ethical issues had already surfaced forcefully within the feminist therapy community at large. Concern had already been raised about incidents of apparent exploitation described to the community by the feminist therapists involved as exemplifying feminist process. The most particular concern within the feminist therapy community focussed on women therapists engaging in sexual and other dual or multiple overlapping relationships with their women clients. These therapists proclaimed that their actions did not create the same problems as when similar actions were done by male therapists to female clients because a power differential did not and could not exist between themselves as women and their women clients. We view it differently.

We in FTI feel that the issue of power is inextricably bound up with ethical issues. The therapist's awareness of power differentials and other such issues are deemed highly significant in the prevention of abuses. We are very much aware that, contrary to the pronouncements of a few, power differentials exist in all therapy, including feminist therapy. The job of the feminist therapist, from our vantage point, is to use that power constructively with the goal of working toward empowerment of the client and ultimately minimizing (even if we cannot eliminate it entirely) our power over the client.

All of us also feel strongly that issues raised by cultural diversity, diversity of sexual and other life style, age, and class also needed to be addressed by specific ethical awareness and concern (Kanuha, 1990). That feminists and feminist therapists were not passive but active in addressing oppression wherever it is to be found also was a pressing message which needed to be incorporated into the FTI code (Rosewater, 1985).

We recognize that the standard prohibitions about dual relationships, which we prefer to identify as overlapping relationships, are not workable (Berman, 1985, 1990). We do not live in a vacuum but are likely to find ourself interacting with our feminist and other activist clients in political settings as well as preferring to patronize feminist rather than other businesses whenever possible. There are many positive aspects to this fact of feminist life, as in the evidence that when therapists are similar to their clients, this is beneficial to the process of therapy, particularly when social class, race and ethnic identity are the issues involved (Carkhuff & Pierce, 1976; Sue, 1975; Vontress, 1971). It is detrimental when the therapist is not aware of the potential impact and does not take any responsibility for dealing with its implications. Realistically, the prohibition against all dual relationships between therapists and clients is unworkable, as the American Psychological Association is recognizing in the softening of its ethical statement on this point in its newly revised code at the behest of rural psychologists and others who work in communities with a sole therapist, a sole dentist and other sole professional practitioners and a small professional community.

As Lerman and Porter (1990b) pointed out: "The simple statement: 'Thou shalt not . . . engage in dual relationships with clients' might be workable if all therapists and clients lived in large cities with large pools of available therapists and if everyone had similar values, or if politics were really divorced from therapy" (page 8). The need to place the responsibility upon the feminist therapist to balance the demands of the real world, instead of denying that they exist, is clear. Michael Gottlieb has proposed a model for how to decide when dual relationships are likely to be exploitative and when they are not, based on the assessment of the degree of power the therapist has in relationship to the client in the first role (concerning nature of the interaction, for example), the duration of the original relationship and the clarity of its termination (Gottlieb, in press).

Other points made by Lerman and Porter (1990b) on behalf of FTI included the recognition that most codes are reactive rather than proactive, that ethics is frequently viewed as a good-bad dichotomy rather than as a continuum of actions generated by the complex nature of human interactions, that ethics codes do not customarily teach how to make ethical decisions, that ethics codes have usually ignored issues especially pertinent to minorities and women and that complaint procedures most frequently focus on legally protecting the professional rather than displaying compassion toward the client.

The process of development of the FTI ethics code is detailed in Rave and Larsen (1990). The authors convey well both the tedium of parts of the process as well as the excitement of other parts during the extended period in which the code was developed. I recall very little difference of opinion about conceptual issues but instead a great deal of heat being generated around emphasis, most particularly focussed around the insistence that racial and cultural diversity and its consequences be addressed as fully and completely as was humanly possible.

The task that we set for ourselves was a large one, that of incorporating feminist values into an ethical code for feminist therapists. The Ethics Code developed by the Feminist Therapy Institute, while not perfect by any means, beautifully expresses in its precepts as well as in the process by which it was developed, our views about what our feminist ethics should be. I have no doubt that the document is and will be a source of inspiration for many.

PRACTICE VS. THEORY

The mere existence of the code is, unfortunately, not enough. We had hoped to develop a process for dealing with feminist ethics issues within FTI that would also explicate our values and ideas. This has turned out to be an even more difficult process than to formulate the code. As in other fairly small professional associations in which the members get to know almost everyone reasonably well, feminist therapists turn out to be as reluctant as anyone else either to confront the therapist who has somehow raised their ethical concern barometer or to initiate and carry through on the organizational, emotional, personal and social complexities of an ethical hearing process.

Napoleon, as I learned while working on another project, was the first one to suggest that it was a bad idea to air one's dirty linen in public. His well known saying emphasizes the value of loyalty and implicitly connects disloyalty with publicity. As an implicit value, this permeates our society. Members of families are taught not to talk about problems outside the family. We feminist therapists have come across this most poignantly in child abuse survivors who have had to overcome this precept in order to gain the therapeutic effects of sharing their unique experiences. Sexual harassment, rape and domestic abuse sufferers have also been subject to the effects of this prohibition on speech. In different ways, this has also affected all whistle blowers in industry, government and the military about corruption issues, health hazards and the like. We as feminists and feminist therapists are not immune to this prohibition.

Before we were feminists, most of today's feminist therapists were socialized first as women in our society. One of women's roles has traditionally been as family (and tribal?) peacemaker. While we learned valuable skills in order to perform that role, we as feminists have learned that those very skills can work against us on occasion. We as women sometimes find that we do not confront when it would be to our advantage to do so, particularly if this involves confronting people we care about. Even therapists who have learned to confront clients as well as to teach clients how to confront others effectively are not immune to the pressures that other feminist therapists can exert.

Within feminism, the implicit prohibition about dirty linen usually has at least two rationalizations attached to it. One is that recognizing that one particular feminist may not be acting appropriately will mean that all feminists will be stereotyped and perceived as doing whatever the inappropriate action is. That is always a major concern of radical movements, particularly those that are attempting to change the mainstream. It can be paraphrased as "What will they think of us?" and "Will it hurt the cause?" I think the appropriate answer involves thinking about how the cause would be hurt in a more fundamental way if we do not police our ranks.

The other rationalization is more personal. In discussions within feminism, the issue of confrontation is often posed as though confrontation in any form would be experienced as personally hurtful by one's sisters. In my experience, this has often prevented us from discussing important views on major issues. It serves as a deterrent to openness perhaps more often than it actually prevents us from inflicting emotional pain upon one another. It allows us to infantilize one another because it implies that we are not strong enough to deal with criticism, anger and/or a viewpoint other than our own. Each of us becomes the caretaker of our sister, whether she needs it or not, but we all lose in the end.

If one looks at the social psychology literature, it is clear that nobody likes a whistleblower in any context (Jansen & von Glinow, 1985). Feminist or not, we all have been brought up to dislike "squealers." Legitimate exposure is, after all, often characterized this way in industrial, governmental as well as feminist circles. Perhaps, not surprisingly, women are less likely to become whistle-blowers at all, according to this literature (Miceli and Near, 1988; Miceli, Dozier and Near, 1991).

The whistle blower literature also tells us that people in industry are more likely to report grievances and complaints when they perceive the organization to be responsive to complaints (Miceli and Near, 1988). At the start of any such process, as is the situation now within FTI, it is most probable that attitudes carried over from other organizations and other settings will still be operative. As the individual organization climate develops, its openness (or lack thereof) will determine later developments.

I have become familiar with the process of ethical complaint within the American Psychological Association as I have helped work toward improving both its ethical code and its ethical processes. Although I have many concerns about the manner in which it deals with ethical charges against its members, it has become clear to me that only a very involved and complex system within a very large organization can handle the very complex and explosive personal and interpersonal issues that ethical charges bring up.

As of this date, FTI does not have a process for implementing its Ethics Code. It thereby relies upon the inspirational message contained in the code itself as a deterrent and has chosen to focus upon ethical issues that arise outside of FTI. There are many to focus on throughout the mental health field and it is a relatively more simple emotional issue for all of us involved to look outside rather than within. The process of developing an ethical process has proved difficult, even more difficult than writing an Ethics Code. Brown and Brodsky (1992) recognized this when they suggested that the process for feminist therapy of developing standards of any kind would be slow and difficult.

In the absence of such standards, the customary ways already prevail. I have seen members of the organization treated disrespectfully without the click of awareness present for the doer. I have seen indirect methods used to convince someone who was violating our ethical precepts to leave the organization rather than dealing with her directly. I have been admonished for helping to bring an FTI member to account for her ethical transgression through another organization. I have seen the difficulty we have had in furthering our own racial/ethnic awareness as an organization and as individuals. None of these incidents feel unusual. I have also seen them occur in other organizations. One difference may be that, while we feminists in FTI may not be as aware as our Ethical Code admonishes us to be, we have made a major public commitment to ending the abuses of the past. I hope that our members will collectively hold us to the fulfillment of the task we have committed ourselves to.

CONCLUSION

Therapists in general believed themselves to be different from other people in that the cultural undertones did not influence them and they therefore were value free until feminists and members of ethnic minority groups forcibly showed that this was not and could not be true. I believe that feminist therapists now need to come to terms with the idea that we have not (and perhaps can not) ever completely overcome the nuances of our cultural training and conditioning in every area of our personal and professional lives. Nevertheless, we need to work toward this goal while actively comparing our words with our deeds, and continually striving toward a better match between our spoken ideals and our actual day-to-day behavior. Consciousness raising, as painful as it is, in this and any other arena is a lifetime job.

REFERENCES

Berman, Joan R. Saks. (1985). Ethical feminist perspectives on dual relationships with clients. In Lynn Bravo Rosewater & Lenore E.A. Walker (Eds.), *Handbook of feminist therapy* (pp.287-296). New York: Springer Publishing Co.
Berman, Joan R. Saks. (1990). The problems of overlapping relationships in the political community. In Hannah Lerman & Natalie Porter (Eds.), *Feminist ethics in psychotherapy* (pp. 106-110). New York: Springer Publishing Co.
Brown, Laura S., & Brodsky, Annette M. (1992). The future of feminist therapy. *Psychotherapy*, 29(1), 51-57.
Brown, Laura S., & Root, Maria P.P. (Eds.). (1990). *Diversity and complexity in feminist therapy*. New York: The Haworth Press, Inc.
Carkhuff, Robert R., & Pierce, Richard. (1976). Differential effects of therapist

race and social class on patient's depth of self-exploration in the initial clinical interview. *Journal of Consulting Psychology*, 31, 632-634.

Gottlieb, Michael C. (In Press). Avoiding exploitative dual relationships: A decision-making model. *Psychotherapy*. Vol. 30, Spring 1993 #1, pp. 41-48.

Jansen, Erik and von Glinow, Mary A. (1985). Ethical ambivalence and organizational reward systems. *Academy of Management Review*, 10(4), 814-822.

Kanuha, Valli. (1990). The need for an integrated analysis of oppression in feminist therapy ethics. In Hannah Lerman & Natalie Porter (Eds.), *Feminist ethics in Psychotherapy* (pp. 24-35). New York: Springer Publishing Co.

Lerman, Hannah & Porter, Natalie. (Eds.). (1990A). *Feminist ethics in psychotherapy*. New York: Springer Publishing Co.

Lerman, Hannah & Porter, Natalie. (1990B). The contribution of feminism to ethics in psychotherapy. In Hannah Lerman & Natalie Porter (Eds.), *Feminist ethics in psychotherapy* (pp. 5-13). New York: Springer Publishing Co.

Miceli, Marcia P., Dozier, Janelle B., & Near, Janet P. (1991). Blowing the whistle on data fudging: A controlled field experiment. *Journal of Applied Social Psychology*, 21(4), 271-295.

Miceli, Marcia P., & Near, Janet P. (1988). Individual and situational correlates of whistle-blowing. *Personnel Psychology*, 41(2), 267-281.

Rave, Elizabeth J., & Larsen, Carolyn C. (1990). In Hannah Lerman & Natalie Porter, (Eds.), *Feminist ethics in psychotherapy* (pp.14-23). New York: Springer Publishing Co.

Rosewater, Lynn Bravo. (1985). In Lynn Bravo Rosewater & Lenore E.A. Walker (Eds.), *Handbook of feminist therapy* (pp. 229-238). New York: Springer Publishing Co.

Rosewater, Lynn Bravo, & Walker, Lenore E.A. (Eds.). (1985). *Handbook of feminist therapy*. New York: Springer Publishing Co.

Sue, Stanley, (1975). Community mental health services to minority groups: Some optimism, some pessimism. *American Psychologist*, 32, 616-624.

Vontress, Clemmont E. (1971). Racial differences: Impediments to rapport. *Journal of Counseling Psychology*, 18, 7-13.

Coyote Returns:
Twenty Sweats Does Not
an Indian Expert Make

Robin A. LaDue

Several years ago I sat in an audience at a major university and watched a non-Native psychologist show slides of a sweatlodge and discuss the healing properties of sweats and other traditional practices. This psychologist professed great respect and admiration for his "Indian brethren" and Native culture. When questioned regarding his expertise and training in traditional healing activities, as well as his right to be presenting sacred information, the psychologist replied that he had "participated in at least twenty sweats." In spite of what this psychologist experienced, twenty sweats does not an Indian expert make.

Coyote Returns is a series of monographs dealing with the issues and needs of American Indians. Coyote is also known as the "trickster" and Coyote stories were used to help teach about rights and wrongs.

Dr. Robin LaDue is a clinical psychologist in private practice in Renton, WA and holds the position of Clinical Instructor in the Department of Psychiatry and Behavioral Sciences at the University of Washington Medical School. She has worked in the field of Fetal Alcohol Syndrome for the past eight years. Her work in FAS has included participation in a longitudinal study of adults and adolescents with FAS and Fetal Alcohol Effects (FAE). Dr. LaDue has lectured extensively in the areas of FAS and American Indian mental health. She specializes in treating emotional trauma and recovery from addictions. She is enrolled with the Cowlitz Tribe of Washington.

Correspondence may be addressed to Dr. LaDue at 1500 Benson Road South, #201, Renton, WA 98055.

[Haworth co-indexing entry note]: "Coyote Returns: Twenty Sweats Does Not an Indian Expert Make." LaDue, Robin A. Co-published simultaneously in *Women & Therapy* (The Haworth Press, Inc.) Vol. 15, No. 1, 1994, pp. 93-111; and *Bringing Ethics Alive: Feminist Ethics in Psychotherapy Practice* (ed: Nanette K. Gartrell) The Haworth Press, Inc., 1994, pp. 93-111. Multiple copies of this article/chapter may be purchased from The Haworth Document Delivery Center [1-800-3-HAWORTH; 9:00 a.m. - 5:00 p.m. (EST)].

93

I wish I could state that this example was a rare exception; however, as this country reaches the 500th year of "discovery," Native people, their cultures, and practices are being discovered once again. Denigration of Native peoples is displayed in the use of Native names and nicknames as team mascots, e.g., the Washington Redskins, the Cleveland Indians, the Atlanta Braves, and the Florida Seminoles. Examples of the less than wonderful aspects of this rediscovery include Crazy Horse Malt Liquor created in the spirit (?) of our revered leader, the so-called men's movement where nonNative men don "traditional" garb, go into the wilderness and *drum* to get in touch with their inner self (Dorris, 1992), and the selling of Native healing practices by nonNative people to other nonNative people (prophets for profit) (W. Willard, April 15, 1992).

An interesting aspect common to many of those who participate in such activities is that they claim to respect and honor Native people. Such a stance is quite reminiscent of the "noble savage" mentality that makes a mockery of Native people as caricatures rather than human beings.

Seeing Native people and their traditional practices in a simplistic, two-dimensional fashion is a continuation of the "Manifest Destiny/Noble Savage" mentality that declared Indian people simply an expendable species hampering progress, similar to the way many people regard the spotted owl. The examples given above are only a few of those that could be cited illustrating the lack of insight, respect, understanding, and acceptance so often displayed towards Native people.

The often tragic realities of Native life include suicide, homicide, alcoholism, Fetal Alcohol Syndrome, poverty, disenfranchisement, and continued fighting against various local, state and Federal governments to maintain sovereign identity. But there is another, emerging reality for Native people today–one of pride, of reclaiming lands, languages, and rights. There is a seeking to learn the old ways, to adapt and integrate the ancient knowledge into ways of survival today. This is a group of people saying "No" to those who seek to steal our children, land, culture, and traditions.

HISTORICAL PERSPECTIVES

Life Before Columbus

When Columbus "discovered" the "New World" five hundred years ago, it is estimated that three million people were already inhabitants (Deloria, 1985). However, despite the plethora of anthropological literature on Native people, it is often difficult to determine exactly what Native life was like prior to the time of "occupation" (or the arrival of Columbus). What information there is often points to what has been called the "Survival Pact" (Walker & LaDue, 1986). The harshness of the physical environment dictated many of the social structures and rules of behavior governing indigenous peoples. For example, in harsh environments, the rules of the Survival Pact were quite strict. Deviation from such rules often meant loss of life, e.g., in the Arctic or the desert. All community members were expected to abide by the rules of the Survival Pact for the health and prosperity of the group.

In more temperate climates, such as California and the Pacific Northwest, the means for survival were abundant and the rules were less harsh. Native people understood the value of their resources and the importance of the land. The point of life was not to "conquer" the land (a very European and now American concept) but rather to respect and honor the Earth (Walker & La Due, 1986). The concept of land ownership and exploitation were alien ideas to Native Americans.

In Native communities, life was centered around kinship groups and clans (Deloria, 1969, 1985; Dorris & Erdrich, 1991, Neithammer, 1977; National Geographic Society, 1974). In many communities, a democratic form of government existed. Indeed, the articles of the constitution and the concept of "one person, one vote" were not European in origin, but based on the form of government present among the five tribes of the Iroquois confederation (Mander, 1991). As with the governing process, religion, spirituality, and healing were practiced with the integration and cooperation of the entire community. Religious ceremonies were not something attended once a week but rather, were deeply integrated into the routines of everyday life. The power of the ceremonies came from the participation of the entire community and from generations of acculturation into that society. Life was generally perceived in a far more circular fashion than in the linear model so prevalent in Western culture (Johnson & LaDue, 1992).

Children were at the center of the circle of life, beloved and adored. The family supported the children and, in turn, healthy children led to healthy families. Families were supported by their communities and, in turn, gave back to the communities. The communities contributed healthy members to the larger kinship group (today's tribe) and vice versa (see Figure 1). It was into this interdependence of healthy communities and healthy individuals that Native children were socialized. This sense of community is still present and powerful today. When two Indian people meet, it is common for them to ask each other "Who are your people?" This often will refer to tribal affiliation and also to family, the sense of being connected with the past, to the present and into the future (Allen, 1983 & 1986; Cameron, 1982; Mourning Dove, 1990; Phillips, 1986; Radin, 1972; Ramsey, 1977; Zitkala-Sa, 1921).

The healing ceremonies were done *only* by people sanctioned to perform them and conducted in accordance with the rules of the Survival Pact. The shaman (or traditional healers) were men and women from the community. Their training was intense: years of study were required–with time commitments similar to the training of psychologists and physicians today. No split was made between the mind and the body, the mind (of course) residing in the body (Walker, 1986). When a community member was ill, the shaman diagnosed and prescribed. If ceremonies were required, they were done in a prescribed fashion, based on generations of traditions, and were conducted with the aid of the entire community (Allen, 1983 & 1986; Cameron, 1982; Mourning Dove, 1990; Phillips, 1986; Radin, 1972; Ramsey, 1977; Zitkala-Sa, 1921; Swimomish Tribal Mental Health Project, 1989).

From First Contact to Self-Determination

The European occupation and exploration of the New World was accompanied by the enslavement, decimation by illness, and systematic genocide of the indigenous peoples. Smallpox, influenza, and measles epidemics devastated Native communities, sometimes by as much as 75% (Dobyns, 1956; Walker, 1986). The conflict

FIGURE 1. The circle of life is comprised of interconnecting circles. To have a healthy community, there must be healthy families and healthy individuals. Anything that damages one circle will affect all of the others.

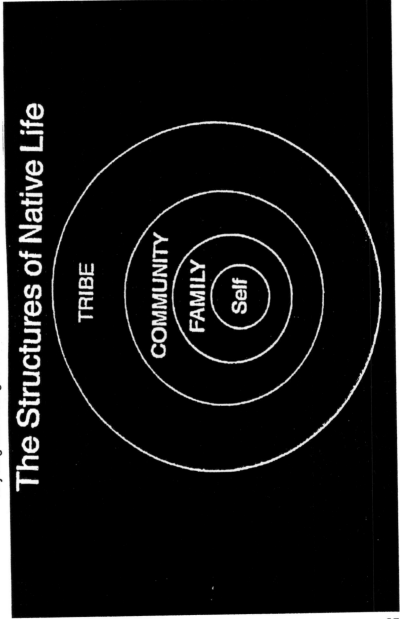

The Structures of Native Life

TRIBE

COMMUNITY

FAMILY

Self

between the indigenous people and "settlers" over land was resolved by the forced removal of tribes and the implementation of the reservation system. A more insidious form of genocide was practiced by the federal government and several of the more powerful organized religions through boarding schools. Native children were removed by the thousands from their families, put into barracks, and divested of their culture, e.g., their hair was shorn, and they were forbidden to speak their language or practice their religion (Gidley, 1979).

For a people whose way of life was based in the kinship group and close harmony with the land, such treatment was spiritually, psychologically, and emotionally devastating. In the 1700's, with the establishment of the fur trade, alcohol was introduced to Native people; two hundred and fifty years later, Native people still have not recovered from this scourge (Mail, 1980a & 1980b).

By the turn of the twentieth century, the Native languages were fading, the elders were dying, and it was illegal to practice traditional religions and healing practices. The federal government, through military action (Brown, 1971; Beal, 1971) and the formation of the reservation system, had forced the tribes out of their homelands into the poorest land of the continent. Legislation, such as the Dawes Act of 1887 which gave individuals the right to sell their land allotments, led to more loss of land which many tribes are now attempting to regain (Tyler, 1973; Wilkinson, 1987). Despair, depression, and loss of the family and community lead to a profound cultural trauma that has persisted to the present.

Self-Determination to Sobriety

The bleakness of this picture remained unchecked until 1934 when the Wheeler-Howard Act was passed, reaffirming the sovereign status of the tribes and allowing the individual tribes to establish their own governments. Tribal councils were put in place to facilitate decisions affecting tribal members and to establish a government-to-government relationship with the Federal government. It should be noted that formal councils, such as those established by the 1934 legislation, were not in accordance with the traditional methods of self-government (Mander, 1991; Tyler, 1973; Wilkinson, 1987). However, the councils did allow the tribes to take more control in becoming self-governing.

When the tribes (which are legal, not historical, entities) were formed it was a common practice for the government to put historical enemies on the same reservation. These historical tribal and family differences and territorial claims make it difficult, even today, for many tribes to take concise action to address the problems of their people. It is important to note that Indian people were not allowed to vote until 1924 (1948 in Arizona and New Mexico)–decades after the end of the Civil War and well into the present century (Wilkinson, 1987). No other group in this country has been so disenfranchised for so long.

After World War II, alcoholism became rampant among many Indian people. The increased prevalence of alcoholism has been attributed to the termination/relocation movement of the 1950's and 1960's which took away land and aboriginal rights from tribes (Tyler, 1973; Wilkinson, 1987). Thousands of Native people were, once again, taken from their homes, families, and ways of life to hostile, foreign urban environments (O'Sullivan, 1988). This was another significant loss heaped upon the already present losses of language, land, elders, family, and culture. Suicide, violence, and homicide all increased to epidemic proportions. School drop-out rates, teen pregnancies, and high rates of unemployment all became markers of the legacy of trauma experienced throughout this country by Native people (O'Sullivan, 1988; Bahr, 1972; LaDue, 1991; Metcalf, 1976; Momaday, 1968; Sarkin, 1978; Berlin, 1984; Weibel, 1982).

In the 1960's and 1970's the environmental movement began. It espoused the connection between the land and people and the need to cherish and protect the environment–values that Native people had known all along. Western medicine began to look at the connection between the mind and the body, knowledge that Native people had never lost. It was also at this time that Indians were, once again, discovered.

As before, it was our beliefs, values, healing practices, and mineral resources that were, and continue to be, stolen and abused. It is hard to say which act of theft is more painful. All over the country nonNative people began to conduct "sweats" and other healing ceremonies to induce "visions." The use of peyote, which was restricted to certain ceremonies among Native groups, became a popular tool by nonNative people to help achieve "inner knowledge" (witness the enormous popularity of Carlos Castenada's writings). However, while mainstream America was discovering the joys of Nativedom, the true aboriginal people of this country were in serious straits (Metcalf, 1976; Momaday, 1968; Sorkin, 1978).

The economic, spiritual, and cultural picture for Native people appeared dark, but a ray of hope began to shine. In 1975 the Indian Self-Determination Act was passed which reaffirmed the right of Native people to choose their own destinies and to practice self-government. The Self-Determination Act was followed in 1976 by the Indian Health Care Improvement Act which documented the dreadful state of health of the country's indigenous people and provided limited funding to begin addressing these serious concerns.

In 1978, two critical pieces of legislation were passed that addressed the spiritual and cultural needs of Native people. The first was the passage of the Indian Child Welfare Act. The passage of this Act slowed the removal of Indian children from their families, communities, and tribes and their placement in nonNative adoptive homes. It established the rights of Native people to raise their own children, a fundamental right never denied to any other ethnic group in this country.

The second piece of legislation passed in 1978 was the Indian Religious Freedom Act. Although the first amendment guaranteed freedom of religion, this right was not granted to Native people. To say that this legislation has put a complete stop to the attempts at termination of aboriginal rights is premature. It is important to note that NO proIndian legislation, other than recognition of a few tribes, was passed during the Reagan or Bush administrations. Indeed, a critical piece of legislation, the Comprehensive Indian Fetal Alcohol Syndrome Prevention and Treatment Act, presently languishes in Congressional committee.

Sobriety by the year 2000 is a goal many Native communities have set and are actively working toward. Many Native people, particularly those in their 30's and 40's, are returning to their cultures; schools are teaching Native languages again (Swinomish Tribal Mental Health Project, 1989). More significantly, Native people are coming forward and demanding to be heard.

Since 60% of the undeveloped energy resources in this country sit under Indian land, it is possible that Indian people may have a powerful economic voice in the future.

In summary, the previous section is a much condensed journey through the past five hundred years. A number of books have been written about historical and contemporary problems facing Native people. However, it is important to present at least a cursory review of these issues because they are the cancers in the backbone of Indian people today. It may be tempting to be caught in the stereotypes that surround Indian people, the myths of the "drunken Indian" or the "noble savage." The reality lies in the middle. It would be foolish to deny that alcoholism, violence, suicide, homicide, and despair are not part of the legacy of being Native. However, these are not simply Indian problems; there are few communities in this country where these problems are absent. What is often ignored, however, is that for Indian people pride, joy, sobriety, glory, and a commitment to survival are also part of our legacy. More Native people are becoming sober; the Alkili Lake Band has decreased its rate of alcoholism from 95% in 1973 to less than 5% today.

It is impossible to be an "Indian expert" merely by participating in twenty sweats. To be truly an agent of change WITH Native people, both on an individual basis and on a larger scale, it is important to understand how we got to where we are today and what our potential is for the journey into tomorrow. The next section suggests positive avenues for nonNative people working with Native people, not in an exploitive manner or with missionary zeal, but with compassion, understanding, humility, and a desire to learn.

IN AND OUT OF THE CIRCLE OF LIFE

The primary problems facing Native communities today are not the horrible scourge of alcoholism, the genocidal policies of the American government, the high rates of school drop-out, unemployment, and teen-age pregnancy, nor the loss of our land. The biggest obstacle facing Native people today is a lack of time; time because we are losing our elders, the last of those who hold our culture, our language, and our connections to the past. It is through our languages, our culture, our spirituality and our faith that we have survived the onslaught of the last five hundred years. NonNative people who come into our communities must understand these critical elements of our history. The following section will provide an overview of the mental health issues facing Native communities. However, these problems should be viewed in the historical context provided and with the understanding that Indian people are determined to make changes. Indeed, many positive changes are occurring.

To understand the cultural and individual trauma faced by Indian communities and individuals, it is helpful to return to the circle of life (see Figure 2). The circle is never-beginning and never-ending, as is the Earth. The day starts in the East as do our lives. The East is the direction of new births and new beginnings. To the South are innocence, acceptance, and the freshness of new life. The South is the foundation of our lives on which we build to help withstand the hard times, the sad times. To the West are strength and courage, more bricks of our foundation. It was, and still should be, the responsibility of the family, the community, and the society to ensure that our children are protected and educated to acquire needed strength and courage. To the North is Wisdom, the most precious gift of all. Trauma takes people and communities out of the circle; healing brings them back (Johnson & LaDue, 1992).

It is trauma that Indian people and communities have faced in the past and face today that have forced them into their own circles of despair, of alcoholism, of sadness, and grief. It is spiritual healing that has begun and must continue for Native people to return to the circle of life.

ISSUES AND OPTIONS
FACING CONTEMPORARY NATIVE COMMUNITIES

Alcoholism, the Symptom, the Treatment, and the Problem: Why Do We Take the Worst of the White Man's Vices and Call It Indian? Indians Never Drank Before the White Man Came (Washington, 1978).

Alcohol, and other drugs, are often cited as the number one health problem facing Indian people today. Studies have shown that

FIGURE 2. The circle of life can be disrupted by any type of trauma. Trauma takes people out of the circle; healing brings them back in.

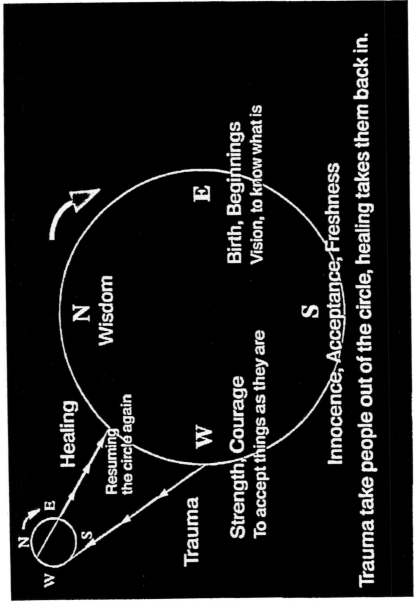

loss of cultural ties and values and increased physical distance from traditional centers of support accentuate the risk of alcohol abuse (Frederick, 1973; Leland, 1978; Loretto, Beauvais, Oetting, 1988; May, 1982, 1988, 1983a, 1985, & 1983; May, Hymbaugh, Aase, & Samet, Shore, 1983b; Silk-Walker, 1988; Streissguth, 1986, 1988; Westermeyer, 1982). Alcohol use increased significantly after World War II concurrent with the termination/relocation movement and the displacement of thousands of Native people from their homes and communities. Alcohol, in many settings, contributes to group solidarity by numbing the pain of grief, loss, and despair.

Alcohol abuse in Indian communities has become a pattern that is passed from generation to generation. The vast majority of violence, suicides, and homicides that occur in Indian country involve alcohol. Alcohol use during pregnancy has lead to an epidemic of people affected with Fetal Alcohol syndrome, a developmental disability characterized by growth deficiency, physical abnormalities, and mental retardation (Streissguth, 1986, 1988). Since healthy communities are dependent upon healthy children, alcoholism and Fetal Alcohol syndrome are disrupting the circle of life and robbing people and their communities of their potential.

Alcohol use, starting at an early age, often under 10, contributes to a continuing cycle of depression, violence, school drop-out, and physical health problems. However, alcoholism among Indian people came AFTER the traumas described previously. Health care providers in Indian country need to treat not just the alcohol abuse but must also work to empower Indian people to make changes on a larger scale.

Mental Health Issues: Depression, Suicide, Homicide, Child Abuse and Neglect

Multiple factors have increased the risk and rates of depression, suicide, homicide, accidental deaths, and child abuse: epidemics; the imposition of the reservation system; the forced removal of Indian children from their families; termination and relocation; and alcoholism and drug abuse (May, 1988; Berlin, 1978; Manson, 1988). Teenage pregnancy, without the support of the extended family, has also increased the hardships experienced by Indian children. It is not that Indian people do not care for their children. The governmental and religious boarding schools that many Indian people were forced to attend robbed Native people of good parenting skills, their sense of family, and their sense of self-worth (Swinomish Tribal Mental Health Project, 1989; Gidley, 1979; LaDue, 1991).

The Loss of the Elders

The most potentially harmful problem facing Native communities today is the loss of our elders. Our elders are the story-tellers, the ones who know. They are our connections to the past and the one's who help set our feet on the right path into the future. Their wisdom comes from generations of knowledge and surviving trauma, e.g., surviving the trauma of the boarding schools. It is because of their wisdom, and the way it was gained, that it is such an incredible insult for someone to proclaim "expertise" and the right to share sacred knowledge simply by having participated in a few sweats.

The language, spirituality, and culture of Native people are so closely entwined that the loss of one may lead to the loss of all. It is for this reason that the tribes have established their own schools and are teaching the language and culture again, to bring a sense of dignity and pride to their children. These are not tools that can be brought into Native communities from the outside nor "things" to be taken upon whim by outsiders. They are priceless gems to be cherished and used in accordance with the spiritual beliefs and guidelines of each group.

Suggestions for "Ethical" Interventions

I have heard, more times than I care to recall, ignorant and hurtful statements made by nonNative professional people regarding Indians. As a professional woman, one who survived the experience of growing up with mixed blood and who also survived the excruciating experience of graduate school, I feel strong enough to confront those I meet who feel free to steal and dishonor our beliefs and traditions. For many Native people who have been abused by the health and social services system, confrontation may not be an option, although refusal to participate in needed services may be–albeit an alarming and potentially dangerous choice.

Therefore, anyone working in Indian country would be well advised to examine closely her or his own beliefs and motives. Indian people do not need any more people who want to "do something" for us, "rescue" our poor children, "save our souls," "share" our knowledge with the outside world or "economically develop" us. Below are some of the approaches that might be reasonable and lead to a more sensitive, appropriate, and ethical manner in working with Native communities (Swinomish Tribal Mental Health Project, 1989; LaDue, 1991).

The Role of the Family

The role of the family in working with Native people is critical. It is usually the family who identifies the patient and determines what problems are important. Often the family will arrive together to give support to the identified patient and to gather information and advice for themselves. Therapists in Indian country need to learn the extended family structure and to work with the natural helpers in the family.

Much of the mental health work done in Indian country is on a crisis basis. When the crisis has subsided, the family may no longer seek treatment. However, the therapist who is persistent and maintains contact with the family maintains credibility and is more likely to be an agent of change. By developing relationships with the healthier members of the family, the therapist can minimize burnout as well as maximize effectiveness.

The Role of the Community

The community sets the standards for acceptable behavior of its members and defines the role of the professional. Despite widespread destruction, a great deal of Indian life is still rooted in the extended family and community. Funerals, pow wows, religious, and spiritual activities all involve participation of the entire community.

The community may be divided along family lines and historical splits. It is important for the professional to identify these lines as well as the community gatekeepers, natural helpers, and power-brokers (Carpenter, Lyons, & Miller, 1985). A wise professional will make every effort to remain neutral along these lines and to establish working relationships with these community members. Knowledge of the history of the community will facilitate effectiveness. Such knowledge can also diminish the risk of seriously offending community members, resulting in a stonewalled professional or, in some cases, a community request for the professional's resignation.

The Role of the Traditional Healer

The role of the medicine person has always been one of wisdom-keeper, healer, and spiritual leader–a role that extends far beyond that of the Western professional. It is often the traditional healer who will make a diagnosis and determine what treatment is needed. The medicine person will conduct needed ceremonies and may, if needed, delegate some responsibility to a NonNative professional. Medicine people in Indian communities are of incalculable value and are regarded in such terms. It behooves nonNative professionals to understand, accept, and acknowledge the validity of traditional healing methods if they plan to remain and work effectively in Indian country (Neihardt, 1961; Wall & Arden, 1990).

The Role of the NonNative Professional

Psychologists, psychiatrists, social workers, and other helping professionals often see themselves in terms defined by the usual professional standards, expectations, and career placements. While much of this is appropriate, NonNative professionals working in Indian country will need to be flexible, willing to make home visits, to serve as crisis counselors, social workers, and therapists. They should also be prepared to act as consultants, community educators, and to work in conjunction with, sometimes as assistants to, medicine people. An ability to accept the legitimacy of traditional healing and spiritual practices is absolutely critical. If a NonNative professional is asked to participate in community activities and traditional ceremonies, respect must be shown. This respect should extend beyond the actual ceremony and include self-restraint in proclaiming expert knowledge of Native culture, and a refusal to share the ceremonies with the outside world without express community permission to do so.

Arrogance and self-proclaimed expertise are NOT desirable assets for NonNatives working with Indians. In fact, humility, acknowledgement of one's ignorance and limitations, and an honest desire to learn are much more useful tools. A practical guide to working in Native communities can be found in the APA *Guidelines for Providers of Psychological Services to Ethnic, Linguistic, and Culturally Diverse Populations* (American Psychological Association, 1990). Professionals should avail themselves of readings, trainings, and consultation to increase their skills as well as awareness of their own possible personal biases.

NonNative professionals may experience professional isolation working within Indian communities. They may also be expected to be available beyond the fifty-minute therapy hour and the nine-to-five workday. The positive side of working in Native communities is the incredible feeling of value that can come from being accepted and respected within the Native community.

SUMMARY

In spite of the historical trauma and loss experienced by Native people, we have survived. As the 500th anniversary of Columbus' arrival approaches, Native people everywhere are turning back to their traditional values, beliefs, and practices (deLeon, 1992; Dietrich, 1992). Today there are over five hundred recognized tribes and Native corporations in the lower forty-eight states and Alaska. Over half of the not quite two million Native people in this country live in urban areas. Indian people now serve in Congress, as teachers, lawyers, psychologists, writers, social workers, nurses, accountants, mathematicians, veterinarians, and engineers.

We have a long way to go in solving our dilemmas and in developing the potentials of our communities and people. Psychologists, psychiatrists, social workers, and other helping professionals can all be positive agents for change. However, to be such an agent, Non-

Native professionals must NOT participate in activities which promote or condone the stealing and inappropriate use of spiritual activities. They need to be willing to acknowledge their ignorance and to *avoid* calling themselves Indian experts. It is considered sacrilegious to use Native practices without community sanctions, or to sell such services. It should be noted that one Native person's approval does not constitute community support and/or approval. The professional who participates in such activities does Native people everywhere a disservice, and demonstrates disdain for Indian ways rather than the respect so many proclaim.

Native people are feeling the crunch of time and the need to become proactive, sober, and united. No longer will we be the "invisible ones." No longer will we stand quietly by and let our bones be displayed in museums, our children be taken from our arms, our ceremonies stolen and sold to line the pockets of "prophets for profit."

We will be heard, in the wind, on the water, and in the quiet dignity of our old ones:

The people speak. Will *YOU* listen?

REFERENCES

Allen, P.G. (1983). *The woman who owned the shadows*. San Francisco: Spinsters, Ink.

Allen, P.G. (1986). *The sacred hoop*. Boston: Beacon Press.

American Psychological Association (1990). *Guidelines for providers of psychological services to ethnic, linguistic, and culturally diverse populations*. Washington, D.C.: Author.

Beal, M.D. (1971). *I will fight no more forever*. New York: Ballantine Books.

Berlin, I.N. (1978). Anglo adoptions of Native Americans: Repercussions in adolescence. *American Academy of Child Psychiatry*, 387-388.

Berlin, I.N. (1984). *Suicide among American Indian adolescents*. Washington, D.C.: National American Indian Court Judges Association.

Brown, D. (1971). *Bury my heart at wounded knee*. New York: Penguin Books.

Cameron, J.E. (Ed.). (1982). *Daughters of copper woman*. Vancouver, B.C.: Press Gang Publishers.

Carpenter, R.A., Lyons, C.A., & Miller, W.R. (1985). Peer-managed self control program for the prevention of alcohol abuse in American Indian high school students: A pilot evaluation study. *The International Journal of the Addictions*, 20, 299-310.

deLeon, F.M. (1992, April 5). A party unto themselves. *The Seattle Times/Seattle Post Intelligencer.*

Deloria, V. (1969). *Custer died for your sins.* New York: Avon Books.

Deloria, V. (1985). *Behind the trail of broken treaties.* Austin, TX: University of Texas Press.

Dietrich, B. (1992, May 23). Festivities evoke area's explorers. *The Seattle Times.*

Dorris, M. (1992, April 21). Noble savages? We'll drink to that!!! *New York Times.*

Dorris, M., and L. Erdrich. *The Crown of Columbus.* Harper Collins, N.Y. 1991.

Frederick, C.J. (1973). *Suicide, homicide, and alcoholism among American Indians: Guidelines for help.* Rockville, MD: National Institute of Mental Health.

Gidley, M. (1979). *With one sky above.* New York: Putnam.

Johnson, D., & LaDue, R.A. (1992). The function of traditional healing: A cultural and community process. *Focus*, Winter.

LaDue, R.A. (1991). Coyote returns: Survival for Native American women. In P. Roth (Ed.), *Alcohol and drugs are women's issues.* (pp. 23-31). Metuchen, N.J.: Scarecrow Press.

Leland, J. (1978). Women and alcohol in an Indian settlement. *Medical Anthropology*, 2, 85-119.

Loretto, G., Beauvais, F., & Oetting, E. (1988). The primary cost of drug abuse: What Indian youth pay for drugs. *American Indian and Alaska Native Mental Health Research*, 1, 21-32.

Mail, P.D. (1980). American Indian drinking behavior: Some possible causes and solutions. *Journal of Alcohol and Drug Education*, 26, 28-39.

Mail, P.D., & McDonald, D.R. (1980). *Tulapai to Tokay.* New Haven: Hraf Press.

Mander, J. (1991). *In the absence of the sacred.* San Francisco: Sierra Club Books.

Manson, S.M. (1988). Adolescent Indian suicide prevention survey project: Phase 1-scientific background investigation and report. Denver: National Center for American Indian and Alaska Native Mental Health Research.

May, P.A. (1982). Substance abuse and American Indians: Prevalence and susceptibility. *International Journal of The Addictions*, 17, 1185-1209.

May, P.A., & Hymbaugh, K.J. (1983a). A pilot project on fetal alcohol syndrome among American Indians. *Alcohol Health and World Research*, 7, 3-9.

May, P.A. & Van Winkle, N.W. (1983b). Native American suicide in New Mexico, 1957-1979: A comparative study. *Human Organization*, 20, 159-179.

May, P.A., Hymbaugh, K.J., Aase, J.M., & Samet, J.M. (1985). Epidemiology of fetal alcohol syndrome among American Indians of the Southwest. *Social Biology*, 30, 374-387.

May, P.A. (1988). The health status of Indian children: Problems and prevention in early life. *Behavioral Health Issues Among American Indians and Alaska Natives: Explorations on the Frontiers of the Biobehavioral Sciences*, 1, 244-289.

Metcalf, A. (1976). From schoolgirl to mother: The effect of education on Navajo women. *Social Problems*, 23, 533-544.

Momaday, N.S. (1968). *House made of dawn.* New York: Harper & Row.

Mourning Dove (1990). *Coyote stories.* Lincoln, NE: University of Nebraska Press.

National Geographic Society (1974). *The world of the American Indian.* Washington, D.C.: National Geographic Books Service.

Neihardt, J.G. (1961). *Black Elk speaks.* Lincoln, NE: University of Nebraska Press.

Neithammer, C. (1977). *Daughters of the earth.* New York: Collier Books.

O'Sullivan, M.J., & Handel, P.J. (1988). Medical and psychological effect of the threat of compulsory relocation for an American Indian tribe. *American Indian and Alaska Native Mental Health Research,* 1, 3-20.

Phillips, W.S. (1986). *Totem tales.* Chicago: Star.

Radin, P. (1972). *The trickster.* New York: Schocken Books.

Ramsey, J. (Ed.). (1977). *Coyote was going there.* Seattle: University of Washington Press.

Shore, J.M., & Manson, S.M. (1983). American Indian psychiatric and social problems. *Transcultural Psychiatry Research Review,* 20:159-179.

Silk-Walker, P., Walker, R.D., Kivalhan, D. (1988). Alcoholism, alcohol abuse, and health in American Indians and Alaska Natives. *American Indian and Alaska Native Mental Health Research,* 1, 65-93.

Sorkin, A.L. (1978). *The urban American Indian.* Lexington, MA: Lexington Books.

Streissguth, A.P., LaDue, R.A., & Randels, & S.P. (1986, 1988). *A manual on adolescents and adults with fetal alcohol syndrome with special reference to American Indians.* Rockville, MD: US Dept. of Health and Human Services.

Swinomish Tribal Mental Health Project (1989). *Overview of the mental health status of Indian communities: Needs and barriers:* Vol. 1-6. LaPush, WA: Swinomish Tribe.

Swinomish Tribal Mental Health Project. *A Gathering of Wisdom.* LaConner, Washington: 1991.

Tyler, S.L. (1973). *A history of Indian policy.* Washington, D.C.: US Dept. of the Interior.

Walker, R.D., & LaDue, R.A. (1986). An integrative approach to American Indian mental health. In C. Wilkinson (Ed.). *Ethnic Psychiatry* (pp. 146-194). New York: Plenum Press.

Wall, S. & Arden, H. (1990). *Wisdomkeepers.* Hillsboro, OR: Beyond Words Publishing, Inc.

Washington, State of: (1978). *The people speak: Will you listen?* Olympia, WA: State of Washington.

Weibel, J.C. (1982). American Indian, urbanization and alcohol: A developing urban Indian drinking ethos. *Alcohol and Health. Monograph 4: Special Population Issues.* Rockville, MD: National Clearinghouse for Alcohol Information.

Westermeyer, J., & Walker, R.D. (1982). Approaches to treatment of alcoholism across cultural boundaries. *Psychiatric Annals,* 12, 434-439.

Wilkinson, C.F. (1987). *American Indians, time and the law.* New Haven: Yale University Press.

Wilkinson, C.B. (Ed.). (1986). *Ethnic Psychiatry.* New York: Plenum Press.

Zitkala-Sa (1921). *American Indian Stories.* Lincoln: Nebraska Press.

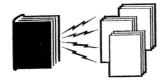

Haworth
DOCUMENT DELIVERY
SERVICE
and Local Photocopying Royalty Payment Form

This new service provides (a) a single-article order form for any article from a Haworth journal and (b) a convenient royalty payment form for local photocopying (not applicable to photocopies intended for resale).

- *Time Saving:* No running around from library to library to find a specific article.
- *Cost Effective:* All costs are kept down to a minimum.
- *Fast Delivery:* Choose from several options, including same-day FAX.
- *No Copyright Hassles:* You will be supplied by the original publisher.
- *Easy Payment:* Choose from several easy payment methods.

Open Accounts Welcome for . . .
- Library Interlibrary Loan Departments
- Library Network/Consortia Wishing to Provide Single-Article Services
- Indexing/Abstracting Services with Single Article Provision Services
- Document Provision Brokers and Freelance Information Service Providers

MAIL or *FAX* THIS ENTIRE ORDER FORM TO:

Attn: **Marianne Arnold**
Haworth Document Delivery Service
The Haworth Press, Inc.
10 Alice Street
Binghamton, NY 13904-1580

or FAX: (607) 722-1424
or CALL: 1-800-3-HAWORTH
(1-800-342-9678; 9am-5pm EST)

PLEASE SEND ME PHOTOCOPIES OF THE FOLLOWING SINGLE ARTICLES:

1) Journal Title: _____
   Vol/Issue/Year:_____Starting & Ending Pages:_____
Article Title:_____
_____

2) Journal Title: _____
   Vol/Issue/Year:_____Starting & Ending Pages:_____
Article Title:_____
_____

3) Journal Title: _____
   Vol/Issue/Year:_____Starting & Ending Pages:_____
Article Title:_____
_____

4) Journal Title: _____
   Vol/Issue/Year:_____Starting & Ending Pages:_____
Article Title:_____

(See other side for Costs and Payment Information)

COSTS: Please figure your cost to order quality copies of an article.

1. Set-up charge per article: $8.00
   ($8.00 × number of separate articles) _____

2. Photocopying charge for each article:
   1-10 pages: $1.00 _____

   11-19 pages: $3.00 _____

   20-29 pages: $5.00 _____

   30+ pages: $2.00/10 pages _____

3. Flexicover (optional): $2.00/article _____

4. Postage & Handling: US: $1.00 for the first article/
   $.50 each additional article _____

   Federal Express: $25.00 _____

   Outside US: $2.00 for first article/
   $.50 each additional article _____

5. Same-day FAX service: $.35 per page _____

6. Local Photocopying Royalty Payment: should you wish to
   copy the article yourself. Not intended for photocopies made
   for resale. $1.50 per article per copy
   (i.e. 10 articles x $1.50 each = $15.00) _____

   GRAND TOTAL: _____

METHOD OF PAYMENT: (please check one)

❏ Check enclosed ❏ Please ship and bill. PO # _____
(sorry we can ship and bill to bookstores only! All others must pre-pay)

❏ Charge to my credit card: ❏ Visa; ❏ MasterCard; ❏ American Express;

Account Number:_____ Expiration date:_____

Signature: ✗_____ Name: _____

Institution: _____ Address: _____

City: _____ State:_____ Zip:_____

Phone Number: _____ FAX Number: _____

MAIL or *FAX* THIS ENTIRE ORDER FORM TO:

Attn: **Marianne Arnold**
Haworth Document Delivery Service
The Haworth Press, Inc.
10 Alice Street
Binghamton, NY 13904-1580

or FAX: (607) 722-1424
or CALL: 1-800-3-HAWORTH
(1-800-342-9678; 9am-5pm EST)